Emotion-Motion Life Hacks
How You Can Enjoy Transforming Your Work and Life for More Success and Happiness

(Text and Workbook)

from YourBodySoulandProsperity.com

Tom Marcoux

Executive Coach

Spoken Word Strategist

Speaker-Author of 31 books

A QuickBreakthrough Publishing Edition

More copies are available from the publisher with the imprint QuickBreakthrough Publishing. For more information about this book contact: tomsupercoach@gmail.com

This book was developed and written with care. Names and details were modified to respect privacy.

Disclaimer: The author and publisher acknowledge that each person's situation is unique, and that readers have full responsibility to seek consultations with health, financial, spiritual and legal professionals. The author and publisher make no representations or warranties of any kind, and the author and publisher shall not be liable for any special, consequential or exemplary damages resulting, in whole or in part, from the reader's use of, or reliance upon, this material.:

Other Books by Tom Marcoux:

- Be Heard and Be Trusted: How to Get What You Want
- Nothing Can Stop You This Year!
- Relax Your Way Networking
- Darkest Secrets of Persuasion and Seduction Masters
- Darkest Secrets of Charisma
- Darkest Secrets of Negotiation Masters
- Darkest Secrets of Film/Television Industry Every Actor Should Know
- Darkest Secrets of Making a Pitch to the Film and Television Industry
- Darkest Secrets of Film Directing
- Now You See Me – Make a Great First Impression - Networking

Tom Marcoux

CONTENTS*

* This book includes even more material.

DEDICATION AND ACKNOWLEDGEMENTS

This book is dedicated to the terrific book and film consultant, and author Johanna E. Mac Leod. It is also dedicated to the other team members. Thanks to Barry Adamson II for editing certain sections.
Thank you to Patricia Fripp, Greg S. Reid, Randy Gage, Dr. Willie Jolley, and James Malinchak for their guest articles. Thanks to Johanna E. MacLeod for insights and for rendering the front cover and back cover. Thanks to my father, Al Marcoux, for his concern and efforts for me. Thanks to my mother, Sumiyo Marcoux, a kind, generous soul. Thank you to Higher Power. Thanks to our readers, audiences, clients, my graduate/college students and my team members of Tom Marcoux Media, LLC.
The best to you.

Use the Real Power of
Emotion-Motion Life Hacks
to Raise Your Life to Higher Levels

"I've tried so many things. I just feel stuck," Cheryl, a new client said.

"I can help you with that," I replied. "How about trying something new, something that cuts away the extraneous stuff? How about focusing and getting yourself to do *the powerful action automatically*?"

"How do I do that?" Cheryl asked.

"You use what I call *Emotion-Motion Life Hacks*," I said.

Authors and researchers have described a "life hack" as any shortcut or tactic that improves one's productivity or efficiency.

I do not talk from theory. As the author of 31 books, CEO of a company with team members in the United Kingdom, India and the USA, I've learned to get a lot done for my dreams—even when my schedule is filled with travel, speaking, and logistics.

The process is about "moving your emotion."

In working with me, Cheryl found the *Keys to Success* that

include knowing yourself, expanding your actions, and expressing what's in your heart.

As an Executive Coach, I help my clients take their lives to higher levels of success and happiness.

I've helped clients prepare for auditions/interviews, build a brand, take a blog from zero to visitors from 173 countries, write a first book, start a business, lead a team, and more.

Now through this book, I serve as your Executive Coach.

This Book Helps You Leap Forward for More Success and Happiness:

My work involves helping clients connect with their intuition.

I ask questions and my clients experience this powerful process:

Insight—>Intuition—>Action.

With this pattern, my clients have an experience of what I call *Catapult-Moments.* The catapult on an aircraft carrier kicks the plane forward *fast.* With Catapult-Moments, you jump forward. You find something new and better. You experience extraordinary progress. Clarity arrives and you feel so alive!

Part of this process helps you **develop skills, strength and stamina**—all vital elements for creating more success and happiness.

I am truly happy to share with you insights and methods under the headings:

- Unleash Your Real Power through *Emotion-Motion Life Hacks*
- A Life Hack to Truly Better Relationships
- Remove Blocks so Prosperity Fills Your Life
- Improve Your Personal Brand for Success and Happiness

- Don't Let Fear Shut Down your Dream! – Move Forward
- Stop Placing Limits on Yourself—Rise to New Success
- and many others . . .

These sections are designed so you can connect with the material and quickly answer related questions.

I use certain phrases so people understand them and remember the ideas. For example, as I coach CEOs, business owners and others, I express my phrase: *"Take command, Focus Your Brand."* Even if you don't have a business, you have a personal brand (it is what you're best known for). Your clarity makes it possible to get more of what you want in life.

Know that answering the provided questions even for just 20 seconds will give you a surprising advantage: You'll learn more about yourself and how to improve your daily actions and strategies in achieving success for your life.

Let's take the next step.

* * *

Unleash Your Real Power through *Emotion-Motion Life Hacks*

Feel exhausted? Or is procrastination killing your dream?

Similarly, my client, Helen, said, "I'm just too exhausted at the end of the day to do any writing."

"I hear you," I replied. "Would you like to explore some options?"

She said *yes,* and we began a process that I call **Emotion-Motion Life Hacks.**

I define an *Emotion-Motion Life Hack* as a technique that you use that incorporates emotion to empower you and create consistent behavior change.

The process is about "moving your emotion."

The idea is the you ARE flowing at your best — through the day.

A – Arrange some hope!
R – Reorganize by energy
E – Energize by principles

1. Arrange some hope!

Get something done for you and your dream on a daily basis. Even devoting just 15 minutes a day to painting a picture or writing a book can fill you with some hope! This will move your feelings and you'll discover that you feel *more* personal energy.

Keep a Progress Log. I log the number of words I write each day. Researchers note that seeing progress (and checking something off one's list) often results in a rise in dopamine in your body. You literally feel better!

Now it's your turn.

How can you devote just 10 minutes today to something that inspires hope in you?

2. Reorganize by energy

My client Helen does *not* feel energized when she walks in the door after a hectic time at her "job to pay the rent."

It's better for her to use her lunch hour well.

She has a bite to eat and writes for 30 minutes during her lunch hour.

The food and time away from work helps her.

She has more energy in the middle of the day than in the evening.

Now she reorganizes her life not by vague ideas. Instead, she monitors her energy levels. Then she reorganizes her schedule related to her energy levels.

Now it's your turn.

How can you do something that brightens your day when you're feeling more energetic?

3. Energize by principles

The essence of Emotion-Motion Life Hacks is using principles that help your function at your best.

Here are examples:

- Keep Score and Achieve More . . . [Use a Progress Log.]
- Courage is easier when you're prepared . . . [Rehearse before a meeting, speech or job interview.]
- Better than Zero*

*Better Than Zero . . . This principle is based on the idea that doing a little bit of some action is better than doing nothing. For example, I have a family member who is in the process of dropping excess weight. I walk with her two times a day. The walks are brief, but her body is getting used to more exercise . . . everyday!

When you use the above principles you have more energy, you get more done, and you feel better about your life. *Your emotion moves in a positive flow.*

In essence, *you move yourself out* of a disempowering low mood into an *empowering* mood. As an Executive Coach and Spoken Word Strategist, I help clients identify what works for them on a consistent basis.

* * *

When you want to rise to higher levels of success and happiness, consider Emotion-Motion Life Hacks. Learn to move your emotion to a more empowering state of being.

You'll get more done, and you'll *feel better* doing it.

What principles would inspire you to have more energy? Will you do some bit of your project (*Better Than Zero*)? Will you keep track of your progress and raise your own morale (*Keep Score and Achieve More*)? Will you rehearse (*Courage is easier when you're prepared*)? Will you use some other principle?

_____

_____

_____

_____

_____

_____

_____

_____

_____

_____

_____

The above section includes:
Emotion-Motion Life Hack #1:
Energize by principles.

Tom Marcoux

Use the Real Secret for Consistent Success (More on *Emotion-Motion Life Hacks*)

"I'm so tired. I thought I wanted to become a professional speaker, but it's so hard," my client Jean said. "I hear you," I replied. "How about we talk about how you can shift yourself out of a down-mood?"

"Yes! I really need that!" she said.

I led Jean through a process I call **Emotion-Motion Life Hacks.** The essence of *Emotion-Motion Life Hacks* is for you to become skilled to *move your emotion* and then you enter an empowered state of being.

The secret of Consistent Success is *renewing your personal energy*, and we'll use the M.O.V.E. process:

M – make a shift (in thought patterns)
O – open to gratitude
V – victory-focus (Daily Journal)
E – engage connection and tracking

1. Make a shift (in thought patterns)

What does it take so you shift how you feel? Shift how you think. It's about thought patterns. Some thought patterns energize us and others don't.

If you start with a phrase like "This always happens to me" or even a question like: "Why does this always happen to me?" you can get your thoughts and feelings into a downward spiral.

On the other hand, I help clients with this process:

Condition yourself to automatically think an Empowered Second Thought.

For many of us, it's natural to have a dark-thought like "if I don't get more clients this month, I'm going under."

I advise my clients to attach this *Empowered Second Thought*: "Replace worry with action." And I invite them to ask themselves: "What small thing can I do now to get myself going in a positive, strong direction?"

Using an Empowered Second Thought and asking an **Empowering Question** is an example of an Emotion-Motion Life Hack.

[A life hack is any technique that increases your productivity or efficiency.]

Now it's your turn.

Take a sheet of paper or a journal and write down your answers to these questions:

a) What is causing you trouble at the moment?

b) What can you do now to get yourself going in a positive, strong direction?

2. Open to gratitude

Feeling down or feeling grateful—for many of us, these two states of being tend to *exclude* the other.

Some people might want to blame our ancestors. The

ancestors who identified negative things in the environment *lived* to have kids. So some authors suggest that focusing on the negative has been encoded into our DNA.

But that's *not* the end of the story. We can condition ourselves to shift our perspective and our focus.

Now it's your turn.

Get into the habit of asking yourself: What am I grateful for? What IS going positively in my life at the moment?

(Write things down. Even Oprah Winfrey writes in her Gratitude Journal every day.)

3. Victory-focus (Daily Journal)

Are you succeeding in your daily life? Is anything working? How do you know?

When I was in college, I went to sleep sad and defeated. Why? I only looked at my to-do list which functioned as a "Guilt-list."

On the other hand, for many years, I have lifted my spirit so I go to sleep happy each night. How? For 2 minutes, I write in my *Daily Journal of Victories and Blessings.* In this way, I see what I accomplished and what "gifts" arrived in my day. A gift (or blessing) can be a surprise phone conversation with a friend.

Researchers have discovered that people need *10 seconds of attention so that any positive thing gets into one's long term memory.*

Ask someone, "How are things going?", and you're likely to hear about the bad things of the day.

Instead, **condition yourself to reply: "Something good that happened was...."**

Now it's your turn.

How will you write down the positive experiences of your day? Will you devote even just 2 minutes to review the good things of your life on a daily basis?

4. Engage connection and tracking

Many of us have heard that we need to track our behaviors so we can improve our performance. There is a classic phrase: "If you can't measure it, you can't improve it."

That is true. Still, when I talk about Emotion-Motion Life Hacks, I make certain to include the emotional component to consistent improvement.

You need *connection* in three forms:

- connection to your heart
- connection to what's meaningful to you
- connection to other people.

Many people fail to keep up their positive behavior changes because their deep emotions are not engaged.

For example, recently, someone asked me about learning to delegate more.

I replied that it's important that we attach a strong emotion to the changes we want to achieve.

It can be as simple as looking closer. One might dislike devoting 45 minutes to train a team member to accomplish a particular task. However, when you calculate that you'll save 1 hour per month **(saving 12 hours!)** by having the team member take over the task, you are likely to become *emotionally engaged.*

Imagine how many more clients a business owner can engage when saving 12 hours.

Further, we want to create connection with the team member. Engage her in understanding the vital role the task has for the team *and also what you can now do better* for the team—now that she has taken on the task.

Express your appreciation and support your real

connection with the team member.

So focus on *both connection and tracking.*

Finally—about connection—I recently gave a talk. I was invited to speak on death. I mentioned that we're invited to live in a "fully-alive" way. Two important elements are included: a) approach each moment fresh and b) *connect with your values.* I feel fully alive each day because I take action to support my personal values of love, creativity and freedom.

Now it's your turn.

How can you track your behaviors and the results you're getting? How can you strengthen the connections on the Three Levels (connection to your heart, connection to what's meaningful to you, and connection to other people)? What can you do to connect with your deeply-held values?

* * *

Remember, to create Consistent Success, you need to take care of yourself and your emotional well being. In this way, you'll increase your personal energy. Use Emotion-Motion Life Hacks.

How will you make sure that you are consistently connecting with people in your life and building warm connections?

_____

_____

_____

_____

_____

_____

_____

_____

_____

_____

_____

The above section includes:

Emotion-Motion Life Hacks #2:

Use feeling gratitude to lift your mood and empower your actions.

How You Can Really Experience Freedom and Joy (More on Emotion-Motion Life Hacks)

"You don't understand. I can't trust Will. He left me there stranded," Cheryl said, tears in her eyes.

Her boyfriend forgot to pick her up at the airport. This immediately triggered her to not only remember but also, in a way, *re-experience* the day when her parents resolved to get a divorce. They forgot her at an elementary school.

When we replay personal pain, we step out of the present moment. When we get blinded by past pain or future-worry, we separate from anyone next to us in the present moment.

I've developed methods I call *Emotion-Motion Life Hacks.*

The Most Important Emotion-Motion Life Hack helps you *Enter the Moment Fresh.* We're talking about the essence of *freedom: to live your life your way.*

Authors/researchers have described a "life hack" as any shortcut or tactic that improves one's productivity or efficiency.

The process is about "moving your emotion."

When something triggers you to re-experience a past trauma, you are literally not free. You're actually someplace other than the present.

I've actually asked a client: "Where did you go?" When she acknowledged that she was stuck in reliving a past, painful moment, *she was then able to move forward.*

How You Can Enter the Moment Fresh

First, you need to identify when you have *left* the present moment.

The hard part for many of us is to stay aware to how we may be buffeted around on currents of thought patterns that keep us in fear of having more pain.

How to Switch Out of a Past-Pattern

I'll share two methods:
- Condition Yourself with a "Switch Phrase"
- Combine an Energy-Move with an Empowered Second Thought.

1. Condition Yourself with a "Switch Phrase"

Some of my clients use a phrase to switch the direction of their thoughts; they're using a "Switch Phrase." My personal favorite phrase is "Replace worry with action."

Because I'm leading teams in the United Kingdom, India and USA, I'm involved with lots of challenges. I do not stay in a worry-thought for much time. How? Immediately, *my mind turns to "Replace worry with action."* Sometimes, the good action is to "get more information" or "develop a plan." Former CEO of the Walt Disney Company, Michael Eisner said that once he and his doctors had a plan in place for his by-pass surgery and steps of recovery, he felt better! It was simply a matter of implementing the plan.

2. Combine an Energy-Move with an *Empowered Second Thought.*

If I feel tired but still I need to grade graduate students' papers, *I tap my closed fist on my right thigh as I say, "I can do this!"* Tapping my fist is an "Energy-Move." My phrase "I can do this!" directs my thinking and feeling into an empowered state of being.

I rise from a low mood thought of "I'm tired" to the energized level of "I can do this!"

"I'm tired is the *first* thought, and "I can do this!" is the *Empowered Second Thought.*

* * *

When you want to experience more moments of real freedom, use the Emotion-Motion Life Hacks that I've shared:

- Condition Yourself with a "Switch Phrase"
- Combine a Physical Move with an *Empowered Second Thought*

For more about Emotion-Motion Life Hacks, see my 1.7 min. video at YouTube.com (type in "Tom Marcoux Emotion-Motion Life Hacks").

What "Switch Phrase" would work for you—so you switch the direction of your thoughts? Would you use the phrase "Replace worry with action"?

_____

_____

_____

_____

_____

_____

_____

_____

The above section includes:
Emotion-Motion Life Hack #3:
Replace worry with action.

Improve Your Personal Brand for Success and Happiness (The "Big Power Life Hack")

"What can I do now to enhance my career and earn more money?" my client Alicia asked.

"Improve your personal brand so people know you, trust you and say 'yes!' to you," I replied.

The *Big Power Life Hack* is to really focus on and improve your personal brand.

Your Personal Brand is the answer to "What are you best known for?"

Your personal brand is a promise of performance. It is how people can put you into a category in their mind.

People do business with those whom they find trustworthy. Additionally, it's important that the person likes you. We like people whom we can count on.

With my clients and college students, I emphasize the elements of a powerful personal brand. I introduce them to what I call "T.H.O.R."

T – trustworthy
H – helpful
O – organized
R – respectful

Imagine how much cooperation you'll get when people find you to be trustworthy, helpful, organized and respectful.

Now it's your turn.

Think of stories when you demonstrated how you helped people. Do the same process for trustworthy, organized, and respectful. Talk about positive experiences people have had with you and how you came through for them.

* * * * * *

For small business owners, it's great to streamline your words so you say memorable things. The following details further help you develop your powerful personal brand.

I guide my clients with the C.A.N. process:

C – call on a catchphrase
A – answer "what do you do?"
N – "niche" yourself

1. Call on a Catchphrase

In marketing, catchphrases are used often so that people understand what the product is.

Years later, I still remember "Zestfully clean"—a catchphrase that sold a lot of bath soap.

Here are examples of catchphrases that people use to clarify the value they bring to the workplace:

• I get the job done.

• People trust me.
• I find hidden profits.

In giving a speech, one can repeat one's catchphrase.

Here's an example, a small business owner could get the audience to remember her catchphrase by repeating it three times: "... that's because 'people trust me.'"

She could even prompt the audience and say, "My client called me to handle the situation. That's because . . ." And the audience responds, "People trust you."

Here's another example. My catchphrase is: *Take Command, Focus Your Brand*.

Finally, in my work as an Executive Coach, I use my catchphrase: "You will achieve more than you believe." This catchphrase works well for me because I have consistently helped people stretch, grow and excel.

2. Answer "what do you do?"

It's vital that you get clear about what you're doing and how you help people accomplish their goals.

You'll do better when you can boil the details to simple phrases that you memorize.

For example, at a networking event, people ask me, "What do you do?"

My answer: I help people create High Trust Relationships so they gain more success and the Golden Yes.

Then the new person and I discuss what a Golden Yes means for their life and career. It might mean "Yes, I'll hire you" or "Yes, I'll buy your product" or even "Yes, I'll marry you."

3. "Niche" yourself

In my work with coaches and small business owners, they

often come to me and ask, "I'm confused. How do I find the right niche for me and my business?"

I've developed *4 Power Question to Uncover Your Niche.*
I emphasize the *3 W's of finding your niche.*

1. **Who** do you want to serve?
2. **Where** is the fun?
3. In **What** ways is the target market most like you?
4. How do you heal them and heal a part of you?

(The fourth question often helps a coach/small business owner connect with her passion. For example, years ago, I realized that I was not asking for referrals. I had fears about asking too soon, of breaking rapport, or of imposing on someone. This led me to teach the workshop/keynote address *Get Clients Fearlessly.* You can see how I help others because I've learned to overcome a problem in my own life.)

Now it's your turn.

Look over the above elements of building and improving your personal brand.

Get help. Talk with your friends. Consider hiring a coach.

When you're vague, the potential client is vague about you.

Improve your personal brand and open the floodgates for more success and happiness.

How will you improve your personal brand? What stories will you focus on (that demonstrate how you are trustworthy, helpful organized, and respectful?

_____

_____

_____

_____

_____

_____

_____

_____

_____

The above section includes:
Emotion-Motion Life Hack #4:
Improve your personal brand.

Tom Marcoux

A Life Hack to Truly Better Relationships

"Damn! I'm so disappointed. He did it again. He just walked past the kitchen where I was cleaning up after dinner. What does he think I am? A servant?!" my friend, Adina said, truly upset.

"I hear you," I replied. Later in the conversation, I said, "I've learned something that really opened my eyes, and which has really helped my sweetheart and me. Do you want to hear about it?"

"Yes!" she said.

Expectations can be a heavy burden like a collapsed roof on a relationship. What's the answer? **Replace expectations with agreements.**

*"Practice leadership by agreements —
not by expectations." – Steve Chandler*

It's natural and human to hold expectations. You buy a product and you expect it to work. You fall in love and expect your life partner to protect you, be kind and be respectful.

Then the pressures of day to day living barge in.

Often, a loved one fails to see what you need because they're so distracted by their own personal problems.

I've learned to quiet down my expectations by asking myself: "Do we have an agreement about this?"

For example, recently, I asked my sweetheart, "Could we have an agreement about helping with the paperwork and shredding personal addresses?"

This was a much better approach that saying something like: "Hey! I do 80% of the grunt work related to paperwork around here."

She did not respond well to comments like that.

Does anybody respond well to pressure or so-called guilt-trip comments?

No!

I've even seen how "Leadership By Agreements" works well.

One of my interns failed two times to get some illustrations in on time—for my graphic novel series *Jack AngelSword.*

I said, "Part of your internship is for me to help you prepare for your dream job. Being on time—or rather—turning stuff in a little early makes you attractive for getting your dream job. **Somehow, our agreement failed here."**

I continued with the intern about the process of setting good agreements.

I did NOT talk about how "I expect you to get your work done on time!"

I talked about how we develop realistic deadlines and part of my job is to help so that the intern has the resources to succeed.

The point about Leadership by Agreement is: *If you don't*

have an agreement, the person is <u>not</u> going to come through.

Many people tend to, like a reflex, resent and rebel against others' expectations placed upon them.

Forming an agreement is respectful. It treats everyone involved like an adult. Carefully forming the agreement brings to light the obstacles that may be in the way of completing the agreed-to tasks.

I invite you to have discussions in which you have agreements with co-workers and even with family members.

Any time, you start to feel upset about someone who has failed to live up to your expectations, ask yourself, "Did we have an agreement?"

What is something that you really want another person to do? How will you gently and positively ask the person to form an agreement? What obstacles might be in the way for the person to come through with the task you are proposing? (Work with the person to form a real and realistic agreement.)

_____

_____

_____

_____

_____

_____

_____

_____

_____

The above section includes:
Emotion-Motion Life Hack #5:
Lead by forming good agreements.

Use a "Miracle Moment" to Overcome Your Fear and Achieve Your Dream!

As I walked on the ocean floor, I took a deep breath and smiled. This was accomplishing one of my Big Dreams.

As a boy, I was thrilled by watching the Disney live-action feature film *20,000 Leagues Under the Sea*. I saw a team of men walking on the bottom of the ocean.

Later, I enjoyed James Cameron's film *The Abyss* which also included deep sea divers.

To get to the point of walking on the floor of the ocean, I had to *overcome two fears* related to *Sharks!* and to the claustrophobia of wearing a diving helmet.

Some days before my trip to the Grand Caymans, I practiced wearing a hood and visualizing that I was fine while wearing the helmet and walking on the ocean floor. *Positive visualization helped.*

I also asked about the presence of sharks, and I was informed that where I was diving sharks found the noise of various ships and the busy port to be off-putting.

Here's what I call the "Miracle Moment" to Really Achieve Your Dream:

It's the moment you connect with Something More Important than Your Fear.

Fulfilling my dream of walking on the ocean's floor was more important to me than my fear.

"Courage is not the absence of fear but rather the judgment that something is more important than fear." – Meg Cabot

Now it's your turn.

Write down your answers to these questions:

What is your Big Dream?

_____

_____

_____

What do you want to do?

_____

_____

What will *Feel Great!* to *you* as you're accomplishing your Big Dream?

_____

_____

What will you be able to do that you cannot do now— when you accomplish your Big Dream?

_____

_____

_____

What fears are connected to what you need to do to accomplish your Big Dream?

_____

_____

_____

What about your Big Dream is More Important than Your Fear?

_____

_____

_____

The above process is connected to what you want *to feel*

when you're realizing your dream.

As an Executive Coach, I often help clients move beyond their comfort zone and to accomplish extraordinary things. I help my clients connect with Big Energy (which is heartfelt) and then they have something More Important than their fear.

Take the time to really connect with what moves your heart. Then, from this foundation, spring up and make progress to accomplish your dream.

The above section includes:

Emotion-Motion Life Hack #6: **Make your Dream bigger and more compelling than fear.**

Six Power Life Hacks

Here I'll share, in a brief manner, Six Emotion-Motion Life Hacks proven to help my clients, audience members and others to get more done and feel better doing it.

We'll use the W.I.N.N.E.R. process:

W – Wake up the "Worst First"
I – Intuit (Top Six Targets)
N – Nurture 3 Levels of Goals
N – Navigate by Goals – "Gold to Green"
E – Energize and "See the 3"
R – Run your own Triggers

1. Wake up the "Worst First"

How can you get the most important thing done each day? Do it when you're fresh.

A paradox in life is: *The thing you most dread will get you ahead!*

Do you need to update your resume?—do it early in the day.

Why? You have more energy and if you work on something early after waking up, you'll often have more access to your subconscious mind.

That's the reason that I often write first thing in the morning.

My clients do these things early in the day:
- writing a book for 15 minutes
- sorting receipts for taxes paperwork
- clearing/straightening one's apartment for 10 minutes

The power of Worst First is that you have full use of your willpower. Dr. Kelly McGonigal, author of *The Willpower Instinct: How Self-Control Works, Why It Matters, and What You Can Do to Get More of It,* notes that willpower is like a muscle that becomes fatigued as the day goes on. That's how you can eat perfectly at breakfast time—but at 11 pm, you might devour donuts! (Keep them out of sight!—or out of the house.)

I guided a number of my clients to rehearse a speech (or part of a speech) *before* they brush their teeth in the morning. Why? *So their subconscious mind can work on the speech all day long.*

Doing the Worst First task early gives you fresh energy and clarity to work on what will most benefit your life.

Write down 4 possible Worst First things that you can do to improve you life. Which one of these will you schedule for early tomorrow? (Which might you do today—to move your life forward?)

_____

_____

_____

_____

2. Intuit (Top Six Targets)

Some people say that they have trouble prioritizing. I respond, "Your intuition knows what's important for you to do now."

Use your intuition: Just before you go to sleep, write down your most important tasks for the next day—your *Top Six Targets.* Then you'll be sure to have a good day, a productive day.

Often, I express it this way to audiences: "Your Top Six Targets: *Two* for you, *Two* for family, *Two* for work."

It's important for you to know the difference between two "voices" in your thoughts.

Voice of Intuition: Expand, experiment, take an appropriate risk.

Voice of Fear: Contract, hide, take NO risks.

Make space to listen to your *Voice of Intuition.*

Write quickly. Jot down your Top Six Targets for tomorrow (or today).

1. Top Six Target (for you)

_____

2. Top Six Target (for you)

_____

3. Top Six Target (for family)

---

4. Top Six Target (for family)

---

5. Top Six Target (for work)

---

6. Top Six Target (for work)

---

3. **Nurture** *3 Levels of Goals*

We often hear about people giving up on their New Years Resolutions. Why? Many of them are *not* skillful in setting their goals. Set a goal too high and it might give you too much fear and cause procrastination. Set a goal too low and you have *no* excitement or energy for the goal.

The solution is to set **3 Levels of Goals:**

a. Good

b. Excellent

c. *Amazing!*

For an author, the goals might be:

In a month:

a. Sell 30 copies of one's book (Good)

b. Sell 300 (Excellent)

c. Sell 3,000 *(Amazing!)*

When we think of *Amazing!*, we get excited. We also need to think on a *whole new level.* How can you sell 3,000 copies?—you cannot do it alone. You need help. For example, authors often team up with other authors. When one author has book about to debut, the others promote the book to their own esubscriber lists.

Now it's your turn.

"Write Down Six" – that is, quickly note 2 goals per topic:
2 "Good" Goals

_____

_____

2 "Excellent" Goals

_____

_____

2 *"Amazing!"* Goals

_____

_____

4. Navigate by Goals – "Gold to Green"

When I was earning my degree in psychology, I wanted to stay in the "positive thinking" approach.

Over the years of coaching clients, graduate students and others, I've learned that people tend to be wired in different ways.

I've found it more powerful to use

Tom Marcoux's *3 Forms of Goals:*

- Golden Pull Goals
- Dark Boot Goals
- Green Tranquility Goals

Golden Pull Goals are the fun goals to talk about. They comprise the goals that *pull us forward*. We consider them our heartfelt dreams.

The truth I've seen is that many of us will only do certain

tasks to *avoid pain*. I call these tasks/goals: **Dark Boot Goals.** It's like having a big boot kicking you in the rear. The pain only stops when you take appropriate action.

For example, a number of people I've talked with tell me that they only do taxes paperwork to avoid tax penalties. Their efforts relate to the Dark Boot Goal of getting one's tax return done and turned in.

I've learned, after accomplishing many things, directing feature films, writing 31 books and more, that only accomplishing projects does *not* yield a happy life. So I added what I call **Green Tranquility Goals.** These are things you do that support your well-being.

My clients have written these goals:

Golden Pull Goals: write a book, direct a feature film, move to New York and get a new job

Dark Boot Goals: complete taxes paperwork, exercise daily and let go of excess weight

Green Tranquility Goals: meditate for 5 minutes in the morning, walk near trees, read a novel in a hot bath.

Now it's your turn

"Write Down Six" – that is, quickly note 2 goals per topic:
2 Golden Pull Goals

_____

_____

2 Dark Boot Goals

_____

_____

2 Green Tranquility Goals

5. Energize and "See the Three"
If you own your own business, the "Vital Three" are:
"This week, how many times did I
a. ask for referrals,
b. ask someone to buy something,
c. have a "sales conversation"?

My idea of "See the Three" relates to what helps people get the Most Important Things done. *You have to a have a simple measurement.*

What gets measured, gets improved. – Robin Sharma

I have several forms of measurement for projects that my company is doing. For my writing projects, I keep a *Progress Log*. For example, at this moment, I have written 22,814 words for this book in your hands. I keep track of the number of words I write each day. Seeing the progress, **keeps me energized and motivated.**
The above relates to my idea "See the 3."
Now it's your turn.

"Write Down Five" – that is, quickly note five things that may be the Simple Measurements that you can keep in a Progress Log. (It's good to write more than three so you can discard that which is not most important to you.)

_____

_____

_____

_____

_____

6. Run your own Triggers

As I work with clients, I hear a lot about their triggers. A trigger is a stimulus in the environment that gets you into automatic behavior.

Here's an example: Susan returns home from work. She sees that her boyfriend has left a bag of cookies on the table. Instantly, she is triggered to "reflexively" pull three cookies from the bag and eat them. She soon regrets that action.

My point is that we can take conscious control of creating better habits and what I call "trigger-sequences." Many times we're triggered and we act automatically—and harvest bad consequences.

We can turn this around. Our efforts to empower ourselves can be helped with this distinction:

Set the Positive Trigger when the situation is COOL –
so you act automatically when the situation is HOT.

This is a prime example of an Emotion-Motion Life Hack. You take into account the emotional component of creating empowering personal growth and change.

List Three of Your Triggers – list the behavior you do

NOT like associated with that Trigger.

Trigger #1 (and troublesome behavior)

Trigger #2 (and troublesome behavior)

Trigger #3 (and troublesome behavior)

We use the follow pattern:

Set Your Positive Trigger ==> Convert the situation from automatic harmful behavior to *Automatic Empowering Behavior*

[Example: *Positive Trigger:* See treadmill upon returning home from work. *New Automatic Empowering Behavior:* Toss jacket on the coach and walk on the treadmill for 15 minutes.]

1. New positive trigger plus New Automatic Empowering Behavior

---

2. New positive trigger plus New Automatic Empowering Behavior

---

---

3. New positive trigger plus New Automatic Empowering Behavior

---

The above section includes the following
Emotion-Motion Life Hacks #7 through #12

W – Wake up the "Worst First"
I – Intuit (Top Six Targets)
N – Nurture 3 Levels of Goals
N – Navigate by Goals – "Gold to Green"
E – Energize and "See the 3"
R – Run your own Triggers

Life Hack for Dealing with Grief and Tough Times

Many joyful moments to you as you go through your days.

Recently, one of my Facebook friends reminded me of something I wrote that we can use during the holidays (and other times):

"My own mentors have shown me that when one is confronted by grief and tough decisions, it is helpful to use some principles.

Only in your heart and intuition—and perhaps, during times of quiet and prayer, you may find some helpful thoughts and guidance.

Here are some questions:

1) What is the **kind thing** to do? How can I be kind to myself and other people?

2) What is the **healthy thing** to do? What is supportive of emotional and spiritual health for me and all involved?

3) What is the **holy thing** to do? How can I be kind, loving, helpful and supportive to myself and others? What

kindness would Higher Power appreciate that I do?

And for prayers, "...for the good for me and all involved."

many blessings,

Tom

When you're confronted with trouble, what might be the "kind action," "healthy action" and "holy/spiritual action" for you to do?

The above section includes:

Emotion-Motion Life Hack #13:

Use pre-selected questions to turn the direction of your thoughts and feelings.

Discover How You Can Stand Strong and Get What You Want!

When facts shake up and threaten to derail our dreams, we *can* shift into an empowered approach.

However, a lot of people default into a position of allowing facts to serve as a "stop sign." In this mode, people say, "Oh, it can't be done that way. It doesn't make sense." OR "We've never done it that way before."

Walt Disney did not give in to what "made sense."

When Walt said that he wanted to make Disneyland, his wife Lillian said, "Why would you want to make an amusement park? They're so dirty."

Walt countered, "Mine will be clean."

Walt set up a tradition that all Disney team members contribute to keeping Disneyland clean. It's often reported that you can see Disney executives reaching for trash and tossing it away. Everyone contributes to keeping the park clean.

"Disneyland is a show." – Walt Disney

I have been directing films, (then) feature films, and videos since I was nine years old. One thing that happens a lot is: *People like to "put on a show."* **There's a joy in creating the magic of a show.** So start with a vision.

The empowered way to deal with facts that threaten to derail your dream is: Use these facts as a Springboard.

How? Ask empowering questions. I use "G.A.P." as mnemonic device. We look for the "gap" between the troublesome facts.

G.A.P. stands for "Give. Around. Possible."
- What can I **give** people?
- How can we go **around** it?
- What else is **possible**?

1. What can I give people?

What kind of experience can you give people? Walt Disney gave Disney Team members the feeling of "putting on a show." Disney team member are called Cast Members, and the park attendees are known as "Guests." Disney Team members feel part of a cause—that of giving people indelible happy memories. How great!

So you can give your team members a vision and purpose.

And, you can give prospective customers something extra. I have a phrase: "customer delight," which is built on something extra and surprising.

2. How can we go around it?

Many solutions arise when we stop slamming head-on into the problem. For example, the martial art Aikido is about side-stepping out of the way of the opponent's force. Then the Aikido master guides the opponent into the ground—in the direction he was already going.

How can you go around the problem—or over it—or

under it?

The idea is to free up your thinking.

For example, numerous people are dealing with the startup funding problem by going directly to their target market through crowdfunding.

Instead of the old fashion way of trying to convince venture capitalists of your project's merit, go directly to the fan base and say, "We want to create this for you."

For example, filmmakers wanted to make a *Veronica Mars* feature film. Through crowdfunding, they raised $5.7 million with 91,585 backers.

The above is an example of going around the studio system and reaching directly to a fan base.

3. What else is possible?

Keep asking "what else is possible?" if you hit a roadblock.

For example, Steve Niles had a project called *30 Days of Night*. He pitched it as a comic book, then as a film. With both versions, no one was interested.

Steve then pitched the material as a comic book mini-series. Once the project did well as a comic book mini-series, movie studios bid in the **$1 million** range for rights to make movies from the material.

A lot of people get stuck in "talking about history." When someone says, "That will never work," they're talking from *looking in the rear-view mirror* ("about history").

Your best opportunities are occurring NOW and in the Future.

* * *

Remember this:

Let facts serve as a Springboard, *not* a Stop Sign.

Use these empowering questions to jump start your

thoughts:
- What can I **give** people?
- How can we go **around** it?
- What else is **possible**?

Questions help us open our perception to new positive possibilities.

How can you take a new approach to your project? What can you *give* people? How can you go *around* obstacles? What else is *possible*?

_____

_____

_____

_____

_____

_____

_____

_____

_____

_____

_____

The above section includes:
Emotion-Motion Life Hack #14:
Open your thoughts to new possibilities: Think of what you can give, how you can go around obstacles and what else could be possible.

Tom Marcoux

Remove Blocks so Prosperity Fills Your Life

"What can remove the blocks so prosperity increases in my life?" my client, Allen, asked.

"Fear is the big block for many people. I'll help you quiet down fear and leap forward," I replied.

To open up the floodgates for prosperity, I help my clients take action in four critical areas, and I use the label "R.I.S.E." to make the process memorable. Making a great plan that includes the *R.I.S.E. elements* can quiet down your fear and help you take effective action. Additionally, the *R.I.S.E. elements* lift you to higher levels of abundance and happiness.

R – risk well
I – intuit
S – start creating
E – energize a team and tracking

As an Executive Coach – Spoken Word Strategist, I work

with my clients in-depth to develop their customized plan and implement it.

Here I'll give a brief overview.

1. Risk well

Many of us miss out on bringing in real prosperity to our life because of fear—fear that taking a risk will destroy what we have. The answer is to develop the skills to "Risk Well" (my phrase).

Use these questions to build your plan for identifying appropriate risks:

- Will I grow?
- Will I learn?
- Will I make new alliances?
- Can I avoid "losing the store"?
- Can I make money all the while?
- Does my heartfelt intuition call me to go forth in this direction?

Now it's your turn.

How can you be careful with budgets and resources so you don't hurt yourself when you take an appropriate risk?

2. Intuit

The top successful people I've interviewed demonstrate that they often use intuition. Intuition is like a muscle: If you don't use it, you lose it.

You need to both make space for your intuition, and you need to take action upon your intuition. Intuition is like a friend who says, "You don't listen to me anyway; I'll just shut up."

Instead, honor your intuition.

First, identify which internal voice you're listening to:
Voice of Fear: contract, hide, don't take appropriate risks.

Voice of Intuition: expand, experiment, grow, take appropriate risks

Second, find a way to take some steps forward. Monitor your results. Check in with your intuition again and again along the way.

The thing about intuition is: Intuition gives you Steps 1, 2, 3. You cannot see Steps 18, 19, 20 yet. Still, at Step #3, you can see the next steps of 4, 5, 6. Your perspective has shifted. It's like you've reached the peak of a small mountain, and you can now see other mountain peaks. Intuition will give you *the next steps* to take.

Keep stepping forward.

Now it's your turn.

How can you make time to get quiet and get access to your intuition? How will you take action?

3. Start creating

To bring more income in, you need to create something. You could create a product, a new speech or something else.

Or you could "Create a Great New Impression of You."

You can show how you have enhanced skills, more experience—and you have created new results. When you create such an impression (also known as your *Enhanced Personal Brand*), you can gain a promotion or a raise. [Your personal brand is the answer to: "What are you best known for?"]

Now it's your turn.

What can you create (product, Enhanced Personal Brand) to bring in more income?

4. Energize a Team and Tracking

My phrase is "Use Alliances for Advances."

Collaboration and kindness can create powerful leaps forward.

On many occasions I've helped someone, and soon they will give me vital information or referrals.

Here are what I call **"The 3 Magic Words of Networking": Help Them First.**

Find ways to help others.

Send them a link to a useful article.

Connect people. I often connect someone who needs a service (for example, editing) with someone I trust.

Both people benefit.

Now it's your turn.

- How can you help others?
- How can you build relationships of trust?
- How might you pull people together into a team and get something big done?

4. Energize Tracking

One of my phrases is: "Keep Score and Achieve More."

"Tom, how did you write and publish 31 books?" a number of audience members ask me.

I reply that I keep a number of *Progress Logs* going. I note how many words I write per day. Seeing my progress builds up my personal energy. I get more done.

An old phrase is: *If you can't measure it, you can't improve it.* To unleash real prosperity, you do *not* need only more activity. Instead, you need to track your activities and see what real results are coming in. If something does not work, modify it or replace it.

To know what to do, get the data. Track your results.

Now it's your turn.

How can you track your actions and what results they're bringing in?

* * *

When you develop your prosperity plan to include *the 4 Elements of R.I.S.E.*, you'll bring in more financial abundance and joyful moments.

Remember:

R – risk well

I – intuit

S – start creating

E – energize a team and tracking

When you consider taking a risk, answer these questions:

- **Will I grow?**
- **Will I learn?**
- **Will I make new alliances?**
- **Can I avoid "losing the store"?**
- **Can I make money all the while?**
- **Does my heartfelt intuition call me to go forth in this direction?**

_____

_____

_____

_____

_____

_____

_____

_____

The above section includes:

Emotion-Motion Life Hack #15:

Consider taking a risk by answering vital questions.

- Will I grow?
- Will I learn?
- Will I make new alliances?
- Can I avoid "losing the store"?
- Can I make money all the while?
- Does my heartfelt intuition call me to go forth in this direction?

Learn the Secret to Unleash Real Prosperity — "The Power of 50"

"I'm exhausted," my new client Cheryl said.

"I hear you," I replied, "Based on what you do for your business, it's no wonder."

Cheryl, like many of us who own a business, is working seven days a week. She wonders will she ever be able to have more personal time?

One of my mentors gave me the real solution. He said, "Ideally, you need to shift from concentrating 98% of your attention on just current cash flow."

He was talking about an important point. Many entrepreneurs are so caught up with working IN their business that they are *not* working ON their business. When this happens you don't have a business, "you just bought yourself a job." By this I mean, you have situation in which you only trade your time for money.

The Solution is:
- Build your business so you don't always have to be there.

- Build real business assets.

Here's an example.

As an Executive Coach – Spoken Word Strategist, I need to be right there with my client. In this manner, I'm in the business of helping people *transform* their lives!

Still, every week, I schedule time for:

- My writing related to my next books (I don't have to be there as the books sell in 15 countries)
- Work on my franchise *Jack AngelSword.*

For example, my 29th book *Droids to Magic: Fantastic Tales of Science Fiction and Wonder* recently debuted on Amazon.com.

Droids to Magic features characters from two of my franchises: *Jack AngelSword* and *Jenalee Storm.* These franchises will ultimately include graphic novels, feature films and action figures!

The Power of Exceptional Focus

Do you spend time each week, actually building your business? Or are you—what I called myself years ago—"a little fire truck putting out fires?"

Improve your life. How? Use what I call the **Power of 50."** The ideal ratio of working on current cash flow and working on building your business is 50%-50%. That's how I came up with the *Power of 50.*

It's true that your percentages of working on current cash flow and working on future cash flow will vary week to week.

Still, it helps to keep that idea of 50%-50% in mind.

Ultimately, I want my franchises (*Jack AngelSword, Jenalee Storm, TimePulse, Crystal Pegasus*) to serve so many people that Disney wants to buy my company near the end of my lifespan. I want my work to continue to inspire and entertain people beyond my lifespan.

When you want to make something *Big* happen:
What do you really want to contribute?

What are you doing so that you don't have to work so many long hours as your life goes along?

Remember:
- Build your business so you don't always have to be there.
- Build real business assets.

* For added insight, **view this 1.5 min. video** "Walt Disney, Disneyland 60th Anniversary – Success Strategies with Tom Marcoux" at http://bit.ly/20Beq95 (on YouTube.com)

How can you build your business so you don't always have to be there? What are real business assets you can build?

_____

_____

_____

_____

_____

_____

_____

_____

_____

_____

The above section includes:

Emotion-Motion Life Hack #16:

For wealth: Focus on how can you build your business so you don't always have to be there.

Discover the Power Method to Prosperity

"Damn! I just lost one of my two part-time jobs. Now, I'm in trouble about money," my friend Fred said.

Because he asked, I introduced Fred to the "Power Method to Prosperity." To say it briefly, "Ask Yourself an Empowering Question."

Why does this help? To make more money, you need two things: Clarity and Action.

Let's look at Empowering Questions:

For someone looking for a job:

- How can I design my resume to express something that will make me stand out—and will demonstrate that I will lighten the prospective employer's burden?

For a business owner:

- What can I do today that will secure more long-term customers?

As an Executive Coach – Spoken Word Strategist, I help a number of my clients build a brand from "zero to

Extraordinary." I ask a number of questions and listen carefully to my clients' responses. We also test the ideas in number of ways.

One of the tough things for new business owners is to clearly and quickly express what they do and how clients benefit. As I ask questions, I get the client to fill in the blanks of my formula:

Tom Marcoux's Branding Formula:

I help people _____
to achieve   _____
They feel   _____
My clients say _____

Here's another way to view this:

I help people __(verb)__

to achieve __(results)___

They feel __(successful, relieved, happy about, more effective)___

My clients say: Joe is so trustworthy and smart about marketing that my sales went up 37%. [an example]

Here is an Empowering Question:

What do I do that's easy for me, hard for others and people want to pay for?

This question can help you and me (and yes, Fred!) to consider new ways to bring in income. Think of this: Steve Jobs had the idea that people would pay $0.99 for a song that they could grab for free on the Internet. His idea was new and he had to use his charm and tactics to get music companies to go along. In fact, the Beatles held out for a long time but eventually joined the iTunes fold. People have gained more than 25 Billion downloads of songs from iTunes! I'm participating, too: I have two audiobooks on iTunes myself: *Be Heard and Be Trusted* and *Darkest Secrets of Persuasion and Seduction Masters: How to Protect Yourself and Turn the Power to Good.*

Here's another hint:

One of my mentors said, "If you want clients, you need to talk to them." I used this idea as a springboard: I can talk to prospective clients through videos (less than 2 min.) on YouTube. Each video works as a 24/7 ambassador.

In a 1.7 minute video, I demonstrate how my directing a feature film that went to the Cannes Film market helps me to support clients in Building Their Brand. (You can find my video on YouTube.com when you type "Tom Marcoux Build Your Brand.")

The truth is: a prospective client wants to know you and to feel that you're trustworthy and credible. That's a significant part of the value of a video.

In summary, here are other Empowering Questions:

How can you talk with your clients/prospective clients through videos?

How can you use testimonials to demonstrate you are both trustworthy and quite capable?

To increase your prosperity focus on Empowering Questions, your own clarity—and that you take action.

Write down your answers to these questions:
- How can you talk with your clients/prospective clients through videos?
- How can you use testimonials to demonstrate you are both trustworthy and quite capable?

_____

_____

_____

_____

_____

_____

_____

_____

_____

The above section includes:
Emotion-Motion Life Hack #17:
Use Empowering Questions about how you can increase people's trust in you—to find new positive possibilities.

Don't Let Your Fear Shut Down Your Dream!—Move Forward

Fear can strangle your dream. Just as bad, fear can paralyze you. Many people get stuck because they cannot do something perfectly. That is, their fear of appearing "imperfect" stops them from taking action. Perfection has its place–like when a surgeon operated on one of my family members years ago. However, most things only need excellence. So . . . *set your own criteria for excellence.* That is, identify what you must do to make the project excellent. Let go of perfect. Focus on excellence. How? Ask yourself these questions before you take action on a new project:

1. What must be in this project?
2. What can be left out?
3. How long do you have to work on it?
4. What does the end user expect to find in this project?
5. How can you surprise and delight the end user?

These questions and your answers serve as a starting point for a strategic plan. When you develop such a plan, you can set criteria for excellence.

You decide what is most important for your project.

As an Executive Coach, I help my client set up a strategic plan. Even better, we identify how my client can take important steps forward even while feeling fear.

From interviewing a number of successful people, one theme arises: The successful person took effective action even while feeling fear.

Don't let your fear shut down your dream! That is, do not let your energy be wasted in trying to gain approval from everyone. The fear of loss of approval can paralyze many of us.

Instead of focusing on approval, focus on truly living your life in a joyful and fulfilling way. Your joyful life is built on listening to your heart and intuition.

Your intuition calls you to expand, to experiment, and to take an appropriate risk.

Your fear calls you to contract, to hide, to avoid an appropriate risk.

Heed the call of your heart and your intuition.

I have faced fear many times: acting in feature films, directing my first feature film, speaking to large audiences, singing in a band, recording my first audio book, appearing as a guest expert on television, and other occasions. The idea is to avoid waiting for fear to go away. Instead, seek to quiet fear down a bit.

To quiet down your fear, set your criteria for excellence. Consciously focus on letting go of trying "to be perfect" and "to get everyone to like you" or "to get everyone to like your project."

"The only things I regret… are the things I didn't do."
– Joe Karbo

"Go to the effort. Invest the time. Write the letter. Make the

apology. Take the trip. Purchase the gift. Do it. The seized opportunity renders joy. The neglected brings regret."
– Max L. Lucado

Take a step forward.

I know this to be true. In directing my first feature film, I filmed the first scene until I filmed the last scene. I edited the first sequence until I edited the last sequence. It was all one step after another.

"You don't learn to walk by following rules. You learn by doing, and by falling over." – Richard Branson

Do something today toward realizing your dream.

How will you set your own "criteria for excellence"? Answer these questions:
   1. What must be in this project?
   2. What can be left out?
   3. How long do you have to work on it?
   4. What does the end user expect to find in this project?
   5. How can you surprise and delight the end user?

_____

_____

_____

_____

_____

_____

_____

_____

_____

_____

_____

The above section includes:
Emotion-Motion Life Hack #18:
Set your own criteria for excellence.

Celebrate Wayne Dyer's Life— and Express Your Light

When I heard of author Wayne Dyer's death, I was inspired to write these words and share with Facebook friends:

Wayne Dyer's death, but more importantly, his life means a lot to me.

I'm glad that I was able to meet him and give him a hug. I'm grateful that I wrote to him, and he wrote back and gave me a couple of his books. On the day of his death, I was listening to a video he recorded in 1980. On the day he was making his transition, I was called to listen to his words. Many blessings to Wayne, his family and all of us who benefit from his work. I'm only sharing a few words at this moment. In honor of Wayne, my thought is: "Express your light."

Upon reflection, I thought about *what gets in the way* of our **Expressing Our Light.**

1. Others drown out our Heartfelt Voice

The answer is: *Acknowledge it's your destiny and not theirs.*

Here's a way you can stay strong even when you feel all alone and deeply disappointed that loved ones do *not* support you in your making your dream come true.

Perhaps, like many people, your loved ones are afraid. Maybe on a subconscious level they're afraid that you'll get hurt as you step out of your comfort zone. Or even, they feel uncomfortable being around someone so focused and striving to fulfill his or her potential. Maybe they fear that you'll change and leave them behind when you do succeed on a significant scale. Sometimes we lose friends. Top author and speaker Larry Winget wrote: "Some friendships are like belts. We outgrow them."

Here's an important point to realize: **Other people cannot feel what you feel or intuitively know what you know.** Why? **It is YOUR destiny**—not their destiny. You're the one person who has all the clues and internal signs that your idea is a valuable one.

Perhaps, you've felt the gut-wrenching disappointment when a loved one does NOT support you in your pursuit of something that's close to your heart.

There is an answer that I learned about from my neighbor who races motorcycles competitively. He said, "In motorcycle racing, we're trained with the idea: If in doubt, gas it out." The idea is to "pour on the gas." My neighbor assures me that if there's an irregularity in the road, more gas will help the motorcyclist get over the small ridge.

How can we apply *if in doubt, gas it out?* First, look to yourself for confirmation and energy. Add things that empower you. Often, when I'm writing I'm listening to empowering music. I read empowering books and I see uplifting films.

The point here is: You must take action to keep up your own spirits.

2. Fear strangles Your Connection with Your Intuition.
The answer is: *Identify with your intuition*

Above, I invited you to listen to yourself for confirmation.

Just because someone close to you cannot see or imagine your idea that does NOT mean that they're right! It just means that they cannot feel the value of your idea.

Identify with your intuition and not their fears.

Many things that turned out well took time. For example, it took 8 years and many studios turning down the feature film *Splash* before it was produced, and Ron Howard directed the film. In fact, Disney turned it down the first time, and it was not until Disney created a new division, Touchstone Pictures, did *Splash* (starring Tom Hanks and Darryl Hannah) get made.

A truly famous example is how co-authors Mark Victor Hansen and Jack Canfield held to their intuition and endured 140 rejections before their book *Chicken Soup for the Soul* was published. The *Chicken Soup for the Soul* series has resulted in 250 titles and more than 500 million books sold.

Go by your intuition. Do not rely on others to "have all the answers." So-called experts can be wrong. You may be providing something that is new and different.

How can you recognize your "voice of intuition"?

Here's a quick description of two "voices."

- *Voice of fear:* contract, hide, do not experiment
- *Voice of intuition:* expand, build, take appropriate

risks

Every day and really every moment, we have a choice. Do we grow and expand and step toward our destiny? Or do we contract and hide and let doubters bring us down?

I invite you to nurture yourself and step forward in a steady pace to create new and better in your life.

3. Your fear of loss of approval has you hide your light.

The answer is: *Measure by your heart and NOT their approval*

In a way, I've been lucky that my father is stuck, for decades, in a disapproval mode. *I've learned to listen to my own heart* and ignore his negativity. The truth is he has had no experience related to being an entrepreneur, graduate school instructor, author, and feature film director. Sure, he has opinions—uninformed opinions. And I'm so glad that I ignored his narrow-viewed advice. My life has been so much more of a joyful adventure than merely playing it safe. His constant refrain is "survival." I've replied, "That's not enough. I want to thrive!"

For more encouragement, see my 7 minute video: "How to Believe in Yourself When Others Don't" (on YouTube.com)

Do you have someone close to you who simply does not support your vision?

Walt Disney's own wife, brother/business partner and board of directors were all against Disneyland. Why? There had never been a theme park before. In fact, Walt's wife Lillian asked Walt, "Why do you want to do an amusement park? They're so dirty." Walt replied, "Mine will be clean!"

Walt measured things by his own heart. In fact his first thoughts about creating an amusement park began in 1911 when, as children, he and his sister would stand outside the gates of a Kansas City amusement park. It was not until 1955 when he opened his own gates of Disneyland. Can you hold on to an idea for 44 years? Will you take steady steps forward?

Novelist Greg Bear told me that it took 10 years for readers to discover one of his novels.

My point is that some dreams take several years—and several starts and stops and moments or months of discouragement.

Plenty of people, often those closest to us, will express their doubt. As emphasized in this section, it's really only natural because you are the one who hears your personal and unique "music and vision."

4. Nurture yourself and your vision.

Get coaching and continue your efforts to learn more and more.

Although many of us grieve that Wayne Dyer has passed away; we *can* celebrate the *Light that is in You.*

This world needs people who hold to their vision and persist. Thank you!

How do you know something as a feeling in your body? (This is a possible way to connect with your intuition). Some people say that they have a gut feeling. Other people know to avoid something when their shoulders ache or chest aches. Some people feel a warm sensation in their chest and that guides them forward. How does you body "speak" to you?

_____

_____

_____

_____

_____

The above section includes:
Emotion-Motion Life Hack #19:
Push aside fear and focus on your Voice of Intuition.

Discover the Power of "Lead so I Follow, Speak so I Believe"

How often do you hear someone say something positive about a leader or a manager? Not often. Why? We have some subconscious expectations of what good leaders do. I coined this phrase: "Lead So I Follow, Speak So I Believe."

I have led teams since I was nine years old, directing my first film. I've focused on being a good leader for decades. As a CEO, I currently lead teams in the United Kingdom, India and the USA. I've worked with mentors to develop my leadership skills. Further, as an Executive Coach and Spoken Word Strategist, I guide and support leaders to increase their impact and influence.

"Lead So I Follow, Speak So I Believe" is the experience that I want my team members to have. "I" stands for my team member.

Good leadership is *not* about the leader's ego. It's about making it possible to get things done and to have team members be clear about "the mission and the mighty." By this I mean, the leader shows *how the team member can excel* and "be mighty."

"Speak So I Believe" is about the team member believing that she *can* succeed. It's also about people believing that the project is worthwhile. No one ever got excited by a leader saying, "Come join us. We're doing something mediocre."

"Speak So I Believe" is about **the team member believing that "I can trust *this* leader."**

N – nurture dialogue
O – own your positive language (drop "Loser Language")
W – wonder

1. Nurture dialogue

"Whoever does the most talking has the most fun." – Ruth Reed

Good leadership is not focused on "slick talk." Many of us can see through that. It comes from empowering questions.

When you, as the leader, ask empowering questions, then the team member will have the fun of talking. More than that, you as the leader, will learn a lot about what is going on in your team and in the individual team members.

Use "Headlines" and "Taglines" ("Taglines get the dialogue going.")

An effective leader gives the *headline* like: "I'm now going to talk about three possible solutions to the XY situation."

Then, the leader shows that she or he is open to input by using a *tagline* like this: "After I discuss the three possible solutions, I'm going to open this up. I want to hear your ideas, thoughts and feelings."

How do you eliminate miscommunication and confusion?

When you express a **headline**, the listener **understands your point up front.**

When you use a **tagline**, the listener *feels comfortable and primed to offer useful ideas for the discussion.*

Start in a Positive Manner

As the leader, you set the tone. Do *not* let loudmouth team members start every meeting as a "complaining fest."

Instead, start a meeting with this question: "Who has an appreciation to mention about someone or something that's working?"

2. Own your positive language (drop "Loser Language")

Leaders had better get this fact clear in mind: You're *the leader* not a casual friend.

You know what we do as friends: If a friend wants to complain, we go along. Sure, as a friend, you might be helpful in letting the other person vent.

On the other hand, as the leader, you do NOT let "victim language" or "Loser Language" escape your lips. You do *not* go along with a team member who just complains.

Sure, it may be tough to adapt to a new change required by a shift in the marketplace. But *as the leader*, you come in with comments and questions like:

- Okay. Dealing with this change is going to take effort. *We're good at this.* We're good at adapting and *surpassing.*
- Who has some ideas in how we can do this better?
- What did we learn here? How can we use what we learned to streamline the process?

When Steve Jobs returned to Apple, he *canceled* a number of projects. Jobs said, "Focus is about saying, *No.* And the result of that focus is going to be some really great products where the total is much greater than the sum of the parts."

I invite you to *cancel* "victim talk" or the alliterative "Loser Language." Instead of saying, like a victim, "Oh. It's going to be hard. Oh, it's not fair that we have to change again"—**you take command and, as the great leader, you say**, "It takes effort AND we're good at this. How do we take this circumstance and come back stronger?"

3. Wonder

The great leader is always on top of the numbers (for example, the number of marketing phone calls made this week by the sales team). And the great leader is always *wondering* about: How do we streamline this? How do we solve the bottleneck problem and improve the system? How do we serve the client better and double our reorders?

The great leader is not required to always have an answer. Instead, it's about *having the right questions.*

Inside the leader asks herself or himself:

- How can I express my certainty that this team can handle the situation? How do I reassure team members?
- (If the team must face a tough real situation) How can I tell the truth about this up front and guide the team out of pain and into positive action?
- How can I point out a specific accomplishment Max made and let him know I really appreciate it? (And this will get Max to keep doing the good work. An old phrase is: What gets rewarded, get repeated.)

Outside, the leader asks team members:

- What needs to improve here?
- What's working?
- What do we need to enhance?
- What makes this project excellent?
- What do the stakeholders (clients, board of directors, others) really want here?

* * *

Now it's your turn.

Focus on this phrase: **"Lead So I Can Follow, Speak So I Believe."**

The great leader sets the tone, points to the goals, and leads the team from the front.

I remember directing a student film many years ago. We were running out of time on the location. The camera operator was ill and sitting down. I grabbed the tripod and said, "Everyone, we're going this way." And the team followed me.

Think of a situation in which you need to provide leadership. What would help people believe in you and trust you? How can you use a "headline" to clue the people into your point? How can you use a "tagline" to show that you want to hear the team's ideas, thoughts and feelings?

_____

_____

_____

_____

_____

_____

_____

The above section includes:
Emotion-Motion Life Hack #20:
Improve your leadership: create a dialogue and ask questions.

Discover Secrets to Persist for Your Dream

Everybody was against Disneyland: Walt Disney's wife, his brother/business partner Roy O. Disney and the board of directors. Still, Walt Disney persisted. How? Two things. We begin with "want power."

1. Connect with your Want Power

A lot of people talk about willpower. Often, they say, "I'd lose weight if I just had more willpower." There's something stronger. It's "want power." What do you really want? If you look deep, it's really a matter of a feeling you truly want to experience.

So what feelings do you really want to experience?

Disneyland is a show. . . . Disneyland is a work of love. We didn't go into Disneyland just with the idea of making money. – *Walt Disney*

By the way, as I write this, the 60th Anniversary of

Disneyland celebration is delighting thousands of people. Thank you, Walt for your persistence. (My 1.5 min. video celebrating Walt Disney's Strategy for Success and Disneyland's 60th Anniversary is on YouTube.com.)

Imagine loving what you do. I made my first film at nine years old, and I have been a storyteller ever since. Currently, my team and I are working on my trilogy of graphic novels *Jack AngelSword* (and ultimately a series of feature films). What gets me to work many days in a row, including weekends? Want-Power. I want to experience the joy of collaboration. I want to hear the laughter of an audience responding to a film I make—or a speech I give.

Identify what you really want and find your unique source of personal energy.

As an Executive Coach, I help my clients connect with what they want in their hearts. From this base of powerful energy, we work together to make a strategic plan. And then I support the client as he or she takes effective, consistent action.

So the process is: **Want Power –> Plan –> Effective Action –> Goals accomplished.**

2. Listen and Feel Your Intuition

Where does the energy to persist come from? Your heart and your intuition.

Your time is limited, so don't waste it living someone else's life. Don't be trapped by dogma—which is living with the results of other people's thinking. Don't let the noise of others' opinions drown out your own inner voice. And most important, have the courage to follow your heart and intuition. – Steve Jobs

Your intuition is uniquely your own. No one can really tell you what steps or path will really work. Why? Because it comes from your heart.

I dream for a living. – Steven Spielberg

Many of my projects—a film, a thriller-fantasy graphic novel (*Jack AngelSword*), an audio program up on iTunes—begin with an intuitive thought and feeling. It's like a momentary "dream." It's really a vision of how I'll serve some form of audience and how I'll feel good while creating the project.

If you can dream it, you can do it. – Walt Disney

So take a moment. What do you dream of? What would you enjoy doing? Don't just think of some "reward." What activity would be a reward in itself, that is, what activity would feel rewarding as you do it?

Your work is going to fill a large part of your life, and the only way to be truly satisfied is to do what you believe is great work. And the only way to do great work is to love what you do. If you haven't found it yet, keep looking. Don't settle. As with all matters of the heart, you'll know when you find it. – Steve Jobs

One of the "matters in my heart" is a musical that I'm writing and composing. I'm setting this musical in San Francisco, the city of my birth and many years of my life. I've written a significant portion of this musical thus far. My intuition lets me know that a number of people could be moved by both the music and topics in the musical. This project is something that I tinker with as time permits. I'm more focused on serving people as an effective Executive Coach and Spoken Word Strategist. Still, I keep making progress on my musical.

What type of creativity arises from your heart?

Let's continue with Steve Jobs' comment: "The only way to do great work is to love what you do."

I have a couple of friends who say, "Not everyone can be a Steve Jobs."

That may be true.

However, I've noticed that the people who feel really alive are the ones who put their heart into their work.

And what about this comment "Not everyone can be a Steve Jobs"? What is that? Could it be, for some people, just an excuse to avoid digging deep and finding their own purpose and joyful way of approaching life?

We also face the reality that not everyone is going to do passionate work for a living. And that's okay. Margaret, a poet, may make no money writing poetry. She may work as an administrative assistant to support herself and her son. What if her friend Sarah says, "Why don't you stop writing poetry and learn to write technical manuals? You can make money doing that"?

Instead, let's leave it to Sarah to find her way of living with joyful moments each day. Let each one of us live a life of creativity and expressing ourselves.

Imagine an orange in your hand. You cannot get the juice if you do not squeeze.

How do you get the "juice of life"? Two things: Connect with your Want Power and listen to your intuition.

When you do that, you open up a new chapter—an empowering and invigorating chapter—of your life.

How will you make space to listen to your intuition? When can you have some "quiet time"? When can you devote some time (even just 15 minutes) to something you would feel is fun and creative?

_____

_____

_____

_____

_____

_____

_____

_____

_____

The above section includes:
Emotion-Motion Life Hack #21:
Connect with your Want Power and your intuition.

Tom Marcoux

Stop Placing Limits on Yourself— Rise to New Success

"I feel stuck," my friend Rosa said. After some more conversation, I said, "I've been listening carefully to what you said. And I've noticed something. Would you like me to share it?"

"Yes," she replied.

"It feels like you put limits on yourself, and it's causing you pain," I said.

What kind of limits do we place on ourselves?

Consider if you've ever said the following:

1. I don't have the time.
2. I don't have experience with that.
3. It won't make me money.

1. I don't have the time.

I've learned to fit in creative work in the little nooks and crannies between appointments and work projects. I read a book entitled *The Coffee Break Screenwriter: Writing Your Script Ten Minutes at a Time*. I recommended the book to a novice screenwriter.

You can get a lot done if you decide to get some progress—any progress—every day.

I'm currently completing my 31th book. My work space has a number of posted Logs. I keep a running log of how many words I write a day per project. Any progress is a boost to my morale. I have a phrase: *Keep Score and Achieve More.*

My non-fiction books often begin with my exploring my first thoughts about a topic in one of my blog articles. When you write one blog article per week, it adds up to 52 articles in one year (a significant portion of a book).

Now, it's your turn.

How can you make incremental progress by fitting in some creative effort today?

2. I don't have experience with that.

Try something on a small scale.

The problem is in paralyzing yourself before you even make a first effort.

Just tell yourself: *"I'm going to try an experiment here."* I remember when I first experimented with yoga. I naturally pushed myself and then found that my knees hurt.

So I later tried a *different form* of experiment. I went to yoga class and any time I had the intuition that my knees might be pushed too far, I simply sat down. The class became more about quiet time and relaxing. That experiment worked, and my knees were fine.

Now it's your turn.

How can you try a modest experiment with something that has caught your interest?

3. It won't make me money.

L. Frank Baum tried many things to make money: breeding fancy poultry, running a store (that went bankrupt), producing/writing plays, editing a local newspaper and more. We know Baum for one thing: He's the author of *The Wonderful Wizard of Oz!*

If any of L. Frank Baum's early writing and editing did not "make money" that is ultimately okay. Why? He was *learning* the craft of writing.

Just because you think an activity will not make you money at the moment does NOT mean that you should avoid doing something creative on the side.

Let's note that when musicians Tori Amos and Kenny G did their first music albums—and gave in to the urgings of "veteran producers"—their work did ***not*** capture a wide audience. Later, when both Tori Amos and Kenny G followed their own instincts, then their second albums succeeded. Still, recording a first album *is* useful experience.

The truth is: We do *not* know what will capture the hearts of many in the marketplace. Still, what counts is that we learn and grow by practicing our craft.

Learn to dance well with uncertainty. Life is simply uncertain. That's part of the adventure. Still, do two things so that you continue to grow in expressing your talent and skill: a) Protect the talent and b) guard momentum. You are "the talent" so nurture yourself.

The Hidden Truth about Removing Limits On Yourself:

How do you remove limits? **You fill up your experience of life with that which empowers you:** Habits to focus on courage, compassion, persistence and love. Love? Yes— supporting the highest good for yourself and for others.

The real culprit that encourages each of us to place limits on oneself is: Fear.

I have faced fear often. Every time I do something for the first time (examples: first time directing a feature film, speaking to an audience of hundreds of people, writing a screenplay and more), I have faced fear. I've used the comment from Gabrielle Reece as a guide: "30% of the people will love you. 30% will hate you. And 30% couldn't care less."

I call this the *"30-30-30 Shield"*—that is, if you do not expect more than 30% to love your work, **you are free to explore and grow.** And, if you're prepared that some people will reject your ideas or creative work, then you can find "your tribe."

"A tribe is a group of people connected to one another, connected to a leader, and connected to an idea. For millions of years, human beings have been part of one tribe or another. A group needs only two things to be a tribe: a shared interest and a way to communicate." – Seth Godin

When I was working on my 29th book, I felt excited about my focus on completing a collection of stories. I had a lot of other deadlines going on. But each day, I would carve out some time to work on the stories.

Then and now, I do not place a limit on myself. I give myself the gift of time and space to explore and create.

I invite you to see how you may be limiting your own possibilities.

Realize that by trying various "experiments" with being creative, you may find something different—like L. Frank Baum, who converted stories he told to his children into the classic *The Wonderful Wizard of Oz.*

Let go of having to be "great with the first one."

Many of us simply need to grow and explore—and then find how to "play our own music."

Step forward on *your own path* today.

What self-imposed limits are you placing on yourself? Are you telling yourself that you have no time, no experience or no money? How might you go around these obstacles? How can you do something on a small scale (and build up from there)?

_____

_____

_____

_____

_____

_____

_____

_____

The above section includes:

Emotion-Motion Life Hack #22:

Remove limits by filling your life with that which empowers you.

Use Secrets so You Breakthrough and Live Your Dream!

"Sure, I'd live my dream—if I just knew how to get started," my friend Sam said.

"I can help you with that. First, I'll share 3 Principles that empower you to make massive progress," I replied.

We'll use the W.I.N. process:

W- work it through
I – identify "if in doubt, leave it out"
N – nurture flexibility

1. Work it through

Avoid a lot of wasted time and even pain when you think it through or take a pen and write details down to "work it through." I learned how helpful this process is—decades ago. I have directed films since I was nine years old. I've learned to plan ahead and anticipate what can go wrong—because things go wrong.

For example, I was directing a feature film some years

ago. We were set up on the tarmac where planes take off. (This was before the 911 Tragedies.)

The airport promised me 3 hours. After only one hour, an official arrived and said, "Pack up. You need to leave."

This would have been a disaster if I hadn't planned for it.

The night before, I worked it through in my mind and on paper. It was possible that I wouldn't get the whole time on the take-off tarmac. So I drew my storyboards and devised a prioritized shot list.

So I filmed all the essential moments first.

Then, when confronted by trouble of the unfair shortening of location time, I told my co-producer, "Have the equipment and the extras move slowly and start the 'leaving process.' I'll keep filming."

It came down to me (as a lead actor) and the cameraman getting some final shots.

All the while, my team is saying, "Yes—we're leaving. We're leaving."

My point is "work it through." Figure out what can go wrong and how you can be sure to be okay or even triumph still.

Gail Anne Hurd, executive producer of the TV Show *The Walking Dead* and producer of *Terminator* (the first film of the series) said, "I always have a Plan B and Plan C."

As an Executive Coach, I work with clients so they think through their plans, then save time and resources as they achieve big accomplishments.

2. Identify "if in doubt, leave it out"

When I say "identify *if in doubt, leave it out*," I talking about zeroing in on things that I may have a doubt about. If I have a doubt, it might be my intuition giving me a warning.

For example, I recently spoke to an audience about the

importance of listening to your intuition.

I said, "If your intuition says, 'Don't get on the elevator with that person.' Listen! Stay off that elevator. Some people tell themselves, 'Oh, I'm just being silly. I don't want to look foolish and not get on the elevator.' Do you know what we call people who don't listen to their intuition? Dead."

The audience laughed.

It was probably my timing with the word "dead."

Still, I'm making an important point: If in doubt, leave it out.

In other words, if something feels wrong—do NOT go through with it.

Let's make this clear. **Confidence is NOT comfort.** Even when you're on the right path, you'll likely feel a bit nervous.

That's *not* what we're talking about.

We're focusing on those "something's not right" feelings.

Listen to those feelings.

Many people get into messes and later say, "I knew I should not do that! But I did it anyway. What a bad mistake!"

Avoid wasting your time and resources. Remember: If in doubt, leave it out.

3. Nurture flexibility

To really make a dream come true, it helps to learn to "share the burden."

Nothing is impossible for the man who doesn't have to do it himself. – A. H. Weiler

Be flexible in your thinking. Look at situations from the other person's point of view.

For example, I'm still excited about the completion of my graphic novel *Crystal Pegasus.*

If you viewed *Crystal Pegasus* on Amazon.com, you could notice that there are 10 names on the front cover.

We had a team of illustrators and colorists. They are *all credited* on the front cover.

That may be unusual. Still, people have more fun and devote more productive energy when they know that they will be recognized for their contribution—on the front cover!

Answer these questions for yourself:

- How can you be flexible in your approach to your project?
- How can you get more help?
- How can you do something to truly recognize each person's contribution to the project?

To unlock more opportunities to fulfill your Dream, remember to W.I.N.

W- work it through

I – identify "if in doubt, leave it out"

N – nurture flexibility

Truly enjoy your life; step forward and fulfill your Dream.

How will you develop more flexibility?
Answer these questions:

- How can you be flexible in your approach to your project?
- How can you get more help?
- How can you do something to truly recognize each person's contribution to the project?

_____

_____

_____

_____

_____

_____

_____

_____

_____

The above section includes:
Emotion-Motion Life Hack #23:
Work it through: Write down details and explore the
situation beforehand.

How You Can Step on Fear and Use Faith for Success

A college student, Natalie, asked, "Do you have to do something wrong to create a big success?"

I replied, "I've found it helpful to pay close attention to people who do good things for others and build an ethical, uplifting form of success. For example, Richard Carlson helped a lot of people AND a lot of people bought his book series *Don't Sweat the Small Stuff.* That's win-win."

Later, during that class on being an entrepreneur, I mentioned that there are dark moments for entrepreneurs—moments of self-doubt and fear.

I've learned:

Every success is built on someone slamming their foot down on fear and stepping up.

Sometimes in my life, I've faced fear daily. What keeps an entrepreneur going? Often it's a form of faith that something should be done and you're the one to do it. The truth is: You don't always win in the way you were hoping. Then how can you feel good about yourself?

"Always be a first rate version of yourself instead of a second rate version of somebody else." – Judy Garland

Today, I signed a new version of my Last Will and Testament. How's that for putting things in perspective?

"Let others lead small lives, but not you." – Jim Rohn

So I'm thinking about how it's important for me to be selective about what I do because no matter how you view it, we all have a limited amount of time on earth.

I'm also noticing that it's been one year and one month since a good friend of mine died.

One sadness I have is: during his final years, every month he struggled to barely pay his rent. He had what I called: "A business model that is garbage." I asked him: "Can you go back to your previous clients and ask for more business?" He replied, "No."

He wrote press releases. But writing a good press release does NOT guarantee that some blogs, websites, or magazines will use the press release as the springboard for an article.

So my friend had a line of disappointed clients and little repeat business. That is a "garbage business model."

As an Executive Coach, I'm often called to help a client refine his or her business model. For example, one client asked, "So I need a website?" I replied, "Not a website. Instead, you'll have a blog." My client went from zero to having a blog visited by people from 170 countries. (And this convinced a senior acquisitions editor at a major publisher to champion my client's book.)

So if you're thinking about doing an entrepreneurial project, put some energy into developing a good business model.

* * *

"There's always a way if you're committed." – Tony Robbins

Ask yourself, "Am I fully committed to this project or this person?"

"If you want to be successful, you must respect one rule ... Never Lie to Yourself."- Paulo Coelho

Along this line, my phrase is: "Don't pretend. Extend." (Extend as in "expand your efforts and/or influence.") The idea is to face your fear and really take a good look at the reality of the situation. Then see how you might press on. The idea is to quiet down fear. But do not wait for fear to evaporate. That may never happen.

So be selective about what you're expending effort on. Then devote yourself to taking effective action.

"A rejection is nothing more than a necessary step in the pursuit of success." – Bo Bennett

Along the way, realize that this is an "AND-universe." Do the work, AND enjoy some happy moments each day.

"One of the secrets of a happy life is continuous small treats." – Iris Murdoch

Today, my sweetheart and I went for a long walk. I got her an ice cream bar and had a small bite of the dessert myself. (I was acting in a congruent way for me to stay trim. I wrote a book called *I Left My Thighs in San Francisco: How You Can Use a New Time-Saving System for Weight Loss,*

Exercise, More Energy, and Being Happy While You Drop Weight.

In summary, focus on these points:

- Every success is built on someone slamming their foot down on fear and stepping up.
- Ask yourself: Am I fully committed to this project or this person?
- Support your personal energy and place small treats in your life.

How can you increase your faith in yourself and your project? What models can you follow (in books/audiobooks — by getting coaching)?

_____

_____

_____

_____

_____

_____

The above section includes:

Emotion-Motion Life Hack #24:

Focus on: Success is built on someone slamming their foot own on fear and stepping up.

Step Toward the Fear and
Create the Life You Really Want!

Recently, I was invited to give a speech expressing something important from my life. Here's what I said:

"2 seconds.

This is a time duration that means a lot to me.

In 2 seconds, years ago, I was a stuntman holding onto the hood of a classic, cherry-red, 50's' truck—by my finger tips!—going 57 miles an hour.

In 2 seconds, I saved the life of a little boy.

And in 2 seconds I can share an idea with you that can impact your life and help you improve your life from this moment forward.

The idea I want to share today is:

**Step Toward the Fear;
Use Want-Power**.

Many of us talk about willpower. "Oh, I need more willpower. I need to overcome procrastination."

You see how your will power is strong in the morning, and you eat a perfect breakfast.

But at 11 pm at night, watch out for those donuts!

I've learned that willpower is not as strong as Want-Power.

Every opportunity that I have embraced was based on Want-Power.

With Want-Power, I can go over the fear, around it or through it.

Every opportunity I've embraced involved fear. Writing my books—and fear was attached. Directing my first feature film involved fear.

In fact, I drew 801 storyboards so that I really knew the story and then I could do my best on the set everyday.

The power of Want-Power became really clear to me about a dream I had since I was 8 years old.

When I was eight, I saw a film, *20,000 Leagues Under the Sea.*

And in it, people were walking on the floor of the ocean.

The bubbles rose up from their helmets.

The fish were swimming swiftly about.

This was a magical world that I could visit.

Many years later, I had the chance to walk on the ocean floor. This was my dream!

But then I discovered a fear that I didn't know would impact me so much.

At Walt Disney World, I got on an attraction *Mission: Space.*

You sit in a can that is spun around. And this creates centrifugal force that simulates you're being pressed into your chair—like you were taking off in a rocket.

But there was just one inch from me and the person to my right.

There was 1 inch and a half over my head.

And when they closed the door on my left—there was one inch on my left.

Everything inside me wanted to yell: *Open this can. I want OUT of here!*

This ride was called Mission: Space. I call it: Mission: No Space. [audience laughs]

But I didn't want to make a spectacle.

So I totally concentrated on the TV monitor in front of me.

I would only focus on the images that simulate our rocket ride.

This experience of claustrophobia reminded me of a moment of claustrophobia I experienced watching the film *The Abyss* by James Cameron.

At one moment, there's a guy panicking and we see his point of view. We look out the tiny window of his helmet—while he's underwater.

That moment in the film now had me afraid that I'd have an awful experience when I would be wearing a helmet and walking on the bottom of the ocean.

But then I learned the answer to fear: Rehearsal.

I put on a sweatshirt with a hood. I put the hood on my head and I imagined, I visualized, walking on the bottom of the ocean. I visualized looking out through the window on the helmet and seeing the whole *expanse* of the ocean.

So when I got to the Grand Cayman islands—I did have a great time fulfilling my dream. *I walked on the bottom of the ocean.*

Inside, my inner 8-year-old said, "YeeEESSS!" I didn't know he had an accent. [audience laughs]

I've learned that setting a pattern in my life of
Step Toward the Fear;
Use Want-Power
—has made it possible for me to do well ...

... including in my 20's, I was standing at a bus stop and a little boy was playing with his toy truck.

Somehow he let go of the truck and it went over the curb—into the street.

One idea flashed in my mind: "Hold him!"

I held the boy back from getting his toy, and **a bus smashed the toy truck into a thousand pieces!**

Things I've done have had fear attached.

The fear arrived later. What if I had hesitated? What would have happened to the boy?

Fortunately, I had put into my life this pattern:
Step Toward the Fear;
Use Want-Power

So I had what's called **"a bias for action."**

And I invite *you* to put into your life
this pattern:
Step Toward the Fear;
Use Want-Power

And then *you* can use this pattern so you embrace opportunities—and expand and improve your life.

Thank you."

How can you use *Step Toward the Fear; Use Want-Power*? What do you really want? What fear is slowing you down? How can you rehearse/get coaching?

_____

_____

_____

_____

_____

_____

The above section includes:
Emotion-Motion Life Hack #25:
Step Toward the Fear; Use Want-Power.

PART II:
Insights on
Work, Success and Happiness

Have you noticed that you have more options when you seek out insights from learned people? In that spirit, I'm now sharing insights from learned friends and colleagues.

WORK SECTION:

I am now sharing this article by author Greg S. Reid because how we approach our tough moments (and work includes them) relates to much of the quality of life we experience.

Relaxed Intensity!
by Greg S. Reid

Who wants to follow a caption that would panic with the first sight of crisis or even worse—bail on their ship?

Seems no matter whom it is that inspires us most; the common trait they all possess is what's referred to as relaxed intensity.

This is a person who is calm through a storm, and can maintain their composure through the most challenging times.

Imagine a commercial pilot coming on the intercom and freaking out when experiencing a little turbulence.

The entire crew and passengers would become immediately concerned as well.

The key is to keep calm, hang on and inspire others to follow suit.

This is the sign of a true leader.

Enter our hero—Pem Sherpa.

A young bright-eyed boy who falls in love with a special girl from another side of the mountain and village.

What would be a modern day *Romeo and Juliet* story, they were forbidden to date one another, as one was Buddhist and the other Hindu.

As time drew near when the parents of the love of his life were to marry her off in an arranged ceremony, he takes her by the hand and points to the top of Everest.

"Do we agree that this mountain is the one true god that both our families believe in?"

With an affirmative response, they set on a journey of a lifetime and their climb begins.

As they summit the peak, they remove their oxygen masks and become the first couple in history to exchange their vows on the top of Mt. Everest.

(A feat that has never been repeated.)

Soon, excitement grew to concern, as most people know that it's the way 'down' the mountain that holds the most danger.

Within minutes, Pem's newfound bride looses her sight and becomes blinded by the snow's reflection.

Guiding her down by his side, it would be easy to loose one's nerve, but not Pem, he remains calm under this pressure and shows relaxed intensity in action.

Her vision could not come at a better time as they reach the landing spot for the life flight helicopter arrives to return them to safety.

When tragedy struck.

With a gust of wind, the aircraft literally crashes among the jagged edges and falls before them.

Remaining calm, Pem and his crew pull the crew away from the craft and await the next one to bring them down.

This is where the story becomes unbelievable if not for being true.

Being the tremendous leader he is, Pem keeps everyone together and assures their safety is on its way.

When the secondary helicopter lands a roar of happiness breaks out, until they realize that the crew that came to rescue them had fallen ill due to altitude sickness.

Basically, the first crew had to rescue the second crew that was there to rescue the climbers.

Wild huh?

Point is—no one lost his or her cool. (No pun intended)

They all knew the risks and remained composed to the situations at hand.

In this case, owning and maintaining a relaxed intensity is what kept everyone confident.

Once he and his wife made it to back to basecamp they fled to America where they have enjoyed many years together and have started a family of their own.

Currently, Pem has made a career out of his experiences and now guides groups of people along the same treks he once conquered.

As one can imagine, life is series of challenges and obstacles. The key is to understand that we learn more from someone on one bad day then on all their good days placed together.

It's easy to be happy-go-lucky when things go your direction, yet it's when the chips are down that we discover one's character.

Bestselling Author. Acclaimed Speaker. Filmmaker –
Greg S. Reid is a natural entrepreneur known for his giving spirit and a knack for translating complicated situations into simple, digestible concepts.

As an action-taking phenomenon, strategy turns into results fast and furious, and relationships are deep and rich in the space he orbits.

Published in over 45 books, 28 best sellers, five motion pictures, and featured in countless magazines, Greg will share that the most valuable lessons we learn, are also the easiest ones to apply.

www.SecretKnock.co

Now watch the complimentary full-length feature film:

www.SecretKnock.co/watch-video

Greg S. Reid is also the author of the *Think and Grow Rich Series* ~

Three Feet From Gold, Road to Riches, Thoughts Are Things, and of course... *Stickability.*

* * * * * *

SUCCESS SECTION

I am now sharing this article by author Patricia Fripp because success is built on our ability to quickly make a *warm connection* with new people.

The Heart of Powerful Presentations — Emotional Connection
by Patricia Fripp

To win over your audience, you must connect emotionally. **Use your opening words to establish an immediate emotional connection.** As an executive speech coach when I work with a group, I'll invite individuals to come up to the front and deliver their opening lines. On one occasion, **I had a presenter Stephen, who began to share the facts of his experience of living with deafness since birth.** After he spoke, I felt he was missing an opportunity.

I took him aside and suggested he try a different approach. Stephen spoke again saying, **"Imagine, how my parents felt as the doctor walked into the room and said, I am so sorry tell you this, but your beautiful boy is deaf." He painted a vivid picture of this pivotal moment in his parents' lives.** Whether or not they were parents themselves, audience members were able to emotionally connect with the situation. **You could feel a change in the room.**

You have many theatrical choices in how you open your presentation, but remember that **to foster true engagement, always let your audience know you have their best interests at heart.** Too often, presenters will start with, "I am going to talk about…" or, "What I would like to do first is…" The reality is, **nobody cares about what a speaker** plans or wants to do. **Your audience cares about whether or not your message is relevant to their own interests and concerns.**

I recommend that you record your presentation and have it transcribed. **What we think we say, and what we *actually* say, can be very different.** When you review your presentation, consider it objectively from your audience's perspective—or, even better, ask others to give you an objective evaluation, as I did when I coached Stephen. He had a wonderful story to tell, but it took an outside observer to help him tell his story in a way that would immediately connect with his audience. **You can turn the *"I want to…"* and *"I am going to…"* statements around.** Start with your powerful opening to create emotional connection, and then follow this with you-focused language. For example, "In the next 45 minutes, *you* **will learn four specific ways that** *you* **can transform** *your* **organization."**

Powerful and persuasive presentations connect with an audience on both an intellectual and emotional level.

About Patricia Fripp:

When your message must be memorable, your presentation powerful, and your sale successful, you can't go wrong calling **Patricia Fripp**. She is a Hall of Fame keynote speaker, executive speech coach and sales presentation skills trainer. *Kiplinger's Personal Finance* wrote that one of the best investments in your career is Patricia Fripp's presentation skills training.

Patricia is now virtually everywhere with FrippVT.com, her interactive, learn-at-your-own-pace, virtual presentation skills training. Fripp Virtual Training's Powerful, Persuasive Presentations is a multimillion-dollar, state-of-the-art, web-based training platform that emulates live training and coaching. It is almost as if Patricia Fripp were sitting right there with you.

Patricia often teams up with her brother, legendary guitarist of King Crimson, Robert Fripp, for Fripp and Fripp presentations on "How to Be a Hero for More Than One Day" and "Beginner to Master." Contact Patricia at (415)753-6556,

pfripp@fripp.com, www.frippvt.com

* * * * * *

We'll now learn from this article by author Greg S. Reid because he shares some foundational ideas that help people do better with money, which is one component of material success.

Magnet to Money
by Greg S. Reid

We've all known a money magnet—that lucky person who seems to attract money without doing anything at all. Money is drawn to them, and like Forest Gump's feather, it wafts down and falls right into their lap without any effort on their part. While that might be the illusion, the truth is that some people do attract money, but they aren't "lucky" and they do have to do something to attract and receive it. These people are money magnets because they know how to attract wealth and abundance into their daily lives.

What do they know that other people don't? They know that in order to attract wealth into their lives, they have to look for it, accept it, and recycle it. This three-step process has been diligently followed by the wealthiest and most successful entrepreneurs since the days of Andrew Carnegie,

Napoleon Hill, and Henry Ford. And they are as effective and applicable today as they have been for the last century—in fact, even more so.

Let's take a look at this three-stop process and how you can use it to increase the wealth and abundance in your life.

1. Look for it. Money doesn't grow on trees or fall out of the sky. But wealth and abundance are ever present in our day-to-day lives … we just don't know where to go to look for it. Actually, you're probably looking for the wrong things. Instead of looking for dollar bills, you should focus on looking for opportunities. Yes, wealth and abundance abound and are all around us, but we don't recognize them because they are disguised as opportunities. Opportunities come in the form of introductions, knowledge, networking, mistakes, new ideas and insights into what could be done better, faster, or easier. In other words, stop looking for money and start looking for opportunities. When you open your eyes to them, you'll find yourself attracting the wealth you're seeking.

2. Accept it. You might be thinking that only fools would turn away money, but it happens all of the time. Many people turn down opportunities, not knowing that by doing so, they're actually shutting the door to the very wealth they're seeking, saying, "No thanks, I don't want it." You can attract money all day, every day, but if you don't accept it, in whatever form it presents itself, nothing will ever change. A magnetic money force not only attracts money, but it also pulls it in and holds onto it. The connections you make, knowledge you are offered, and offers for assistance are all money prospects, but only if you accept them with open arms.

3. Recycle it. It's not coincidental that money and recycling are both "green." Both are an integral part of our sustainability, so if you want to sustain and increase your wealth and abundance, recycling is a natural part of the process that will keep it flowing. Recycling can involve many things. When you find something that works, duplicate it. When you attract and accept wealth and abundance into your life, invest a portion of it in different ways to create passive income, where money really will begin to flow into your life without much effort. And don't forget, a large part of recycling is giving back—share your wealth, abundance, knowledge, and success with others so it can be replicated over and over and over again.

Following this simple and tried-and-true process will open your eyes to the wealth and abundance that have always been there, waiting for you to take notice and action. Then you can join those you once envied, wondering what they have that you don't. Like them, you'll soon find that once you open your life to wealth and abundance, it will seek even more ways to find you. And that is when you, too, will become a magnet to money and will begin to live a life rich with abundance and prosperity—a life where you'll find yourself saying, "How can it get better than this?"

Bestselling Author. Acclaimed Speaker. Filmmaker –
Greg S. Reid is a natural entrepreneur known for his giving spirit and a knack for translating complicated situations into simple, digestible concepts.

As an action-taking phenomenon, strategy turns into results fast and furious, and relationships are deep and rich in the space he orbits.

Published in over 45 books, 28 best sellers, five motion pictures, and featured in countless magazines, Greg will share that the most valuable lessons we learn, are also the easiest ones to apply.

www.SecretKnock.co
Now watch the complimentary full-length feature film:
www.SecretKnock.co/watch-video

Greg S. Reid is also the author of the *Think and Grow Rich Series* ~
Three Feet From Gold, Road to Riches, Thoughts Are Things, and of course… *Stickability*.

* * * * * *

HAPPINESS SECTION

In this article by author Randy Gage we learn valuable methods for living our dreams.

Live Your Dreams!

A lightly edited transcript of a video
by Randy Gage

Let's talk about how to live your dreams.

The first thing is you got to chase your dreams. Not somebody else's. We get so much programming at early ages from parents, coaches and teachers, who are very well-meaning people. But sometimes, they get us chasing dreams that are not really our dreams. It may be wonderful that seven generations of your family have been attorneys. Or five generations of your family have been doctors. Or both parents are professors and they would love for you to be a professor.

If that isn't your dream, you're not going to be happy

chasing after it. So let's make sure you know what dream you're after.

The next thing is: Set your intention. Create the goal, the objective, the outcome. I really believe that everything at its ultimate level is energy. Energy can be attracted or energy can be repelled. When you set your intention, I believe you bend the universe to your will.

Know what the end looks like. Be specific. If you say, "I want to be happy, successful, rich," these are just generalizations. There is no way for your subconscious mind to latch onto them and know what they're going to entail. So think of the specific outcome, what your dream would be.

Create a movie script of your perfect day. Write this out and be as detailed as possible. You want to involve all five senses. So you wake up in the morning, feel the breeze, and smell the coffee percolating downstairs. You hear the birds chirping. You write out everything. What is the best day? The day you win the Academy Award; the day your company goes public; the day that your dream comes true. You write out how your perfect day looks like. You carry the script in your purse or briefcase so it's always close by. If you're in line for the bank teller or you're waiting at a red light—any time you have a minute or two—you can look at that script. Every time you look at your script, it reinforces your dream in your subconscious mind. That's what we want to do: We want to program your subconscious mind. Remember that the subconscious mind does not argue, does not analyze and doesn't debate. The subconscious mind just does whatever it is programmed to do.

Be open to detours. Balance making things happen with letting things happen. Sometimes the universe has other ideas for you. You have to be open with the mindset "this or something better."

Create an outcome, be specific, go after it, get into action. But you may need to change course. I have a "three strikes and you're out" thing. If I'm doing something and three times in a row the universe tells me "You're not going to do that," I re-think the situation. Maybe I should be modifying the plan. Or I should change the outcome because obviously what I'm doing is not working.

The most important part of the process is that you're going to get to a decision point when you're going to have to take a risk. You're going to have to quit your job or you're going to have to make a bold declaration. You're going to have to risk losing money. You're going to have to risk somebody's affection or approval. You might have to risk society's approval. *If you really believe in your dream, take the risk.*

More than anything else, I hope that at the end of your days, you do *not* die with your song left unsung.

These are my thoughts on living your dream.

Until next time, peace, love you guys and live rich.

Randy Gage is a thought-provoking critical thinker who will make you approach your business—and your life—in a whole new way. Randy is the author of nine books translated into 25 languages, including the *New York Times* bestseller, *Risky Is the New Safe*. He has spoken to more than 2 million people across more than 50 countries, and is a member of the Speakers Hall of Fame. When he is not prowling the podium or locked in his lonely writer's garret, you'll probably find him playing 3rd base for a softball team somewhere.

Visit Randy at www.RandyGage.com

* * * * * *

We'll now enjoy this article by author James Malinchak because James encourages us to follow the example of some terrific people. We discover that much of happiness rises from how we treat people with kindness and compassion.

Always Be Great Because You Never Know Who is Watching!
By James Malinchak

As a motivational speaker, I'm used to a certain amount of scrutiny. After all, I've made a career out of standing on platforms while thousands of eyes look on and judge what I am saying.

During my experience in Gary, Indiana living undercover on the TV show, *Secret Millionaire*, my identity was a secret, hence the title "Secret Millionaire." No one in the community knew I even had a dime to my name—not even enough money for that cup of coffee with Coach Tony. I was just some guy who simply wanted to volunteer in their community.

The people in Gary thought the cameras following me around were only there to film me and my experiences as a struggling volunteer. They had no idea their day-to-day actions were the real focus of the cameras.

During my first day of volunteering, I expected to be put to work with no special attention paid to me. In essence, I'd just be another face in the crowd. I was wrong. With no idea they would end up on worldwide television, those I volunteered for treated me like family. They continued their normal daily activities of serving and helping others, whether or not there were cameras. They even made me forget about the cameras as we all just lived in the moment.

No one judged or scrutinized anyone.

And here's the most amazing thing—I quickly realized these people weren't putting on a show. They acted out of love every day, and I was blessed to be there to witness it.

That's when it hit me. These people acted the same to everyone, whether there's a crowd of onlookers watching or no one watching at all. It's the kind of spirit that you read about but rarely get to witness.

To these people, I was just another volunteer who was lending a helping hand. It would have been easy to dismiss me as a passing stranger and go about their daily lives without any special regard for me. But instead, they did the exact opposite. With the kind of love and compassion I've really only ever felt from family and my closest friends, I was allowed into their worlds.

And what I realized by watching and observing them, working with them, and being a part of their organizations was that they inspired others with their actions. They treated everybody with the same kindness and compassion, every minute of the day. It didn't matter if it was an outsider who had cameras following him, a mother who picked up her daughter at an afterschool program, or a homeless man on the street. They treated everyone the same and their actions inspired me, the TV Production crew and, eventually, over 10 Million viewers who watched us on ABC.

The impact that such a level of equality and integrity had on me was profound. They are people who have such a desire to help their community and their neighbors that all the usual factors we use to judge others—like social or financial status—don't even figure into the equation. Witnessing this in person, has forever changed my life.

Not one of the beautiful people in the organizations that I volunteered for in Gary knew I was watching, trying to decide who I would give checks to at the end of our time together.

Watching them treat everyone as an equal and treat even the smallest projects with great detail and care profoundly impacted me. These people knew that no matter what the task or goal—whether it was cleaning up streets, helping kids with school work or teaching a young girl how to better dribble a basketball—their intention was to *Always Be Great.* And those three words became a lesson that stuck with me.

If you've ever wanted to inspire others with your actions in business, leadership or life, remember to **"Always Be Great."** Just because no one is directly watching you, doesn't mean that your actions don't count. Strive to **always be great** every day in your business. Strive to **always be great** every day in leadership. Strive to always be great every day in life. Why is it important to adopt this mentality? I'll say it once more: *Always Be Great Because You Never Know Who is Watching!*

James Malinchak is recognized as one of the most requested, in-demand business and motivational keynote speakers and marketing consultants in the world. He was featured on the Hit ABC TV Show, *Secret Millionaire* and was twice named "College Speaker of the Year" (APCA and Campus Activities Magazine). James has delivered over 2,000+ presentations for corporations, associations, business groups, colleges, universities and youth organizations worldwide. James can speak for groups ranging from 20-20,000. visit: www.Malinchak.com

As a consultant, James is the behind-the-scenes, go-to marketing advisor for many top speakers, authors, thought leaders, business professionals, celebrities, sports coaches, athletes and entrepreneurs and is recognized as "The World's #1 Big Money Speaker® Trainer and Coach" teaching anyone who wants to get highly-paid as a motivational or business speaker how to correctly package, market and sell their time, knowledge, experience, expertise, message, personal story and how-to advice. visit:

www.BigMoneySpeaker.com and
www.CollegeSpeakingSuccess.com

* * * * * *

I am now sharing this article by Dr. Willie Jolley because he shares how one simple practice can brighten your days and give you more happy moments.

Dr. Willie Jolley's Thought of the Day: Excellence

A lightly edited transcript of a video
by Dr. Willie Jolley

Here's a thought I've been thinking about all day: excellence!

When people ask me: "Hey, Willie Jolley, how are you doing?"

I always respond, "Excellent! I am grateful and blessed."

Or I might say, "Excellent! I'm blessed and highly favored."

I started doing that from the response I got from a friend I knew who went to the same church as me. He passed away recently, and his name was Deacon Walton. Whenever you would greet him and ask him how he was doing he would say, "Excellent!" He'd say it with lots of energy. It was so amazing how he would do this, each and every time!

I *had* been saying, "Blessed and highly favored; exciting; outstanding." And all of those are good. But Deacon Walton inspired me to go to the next level. From the time I started talking to him I added the word "Excellent!"

Yet most people you ask, *how they are doing*, will say, "I'm doing okay!" or say "I'm just making it!" or, for the more negative folks… they say, "if I didn't have bad luck I wouldn't have no luck at all!" They don't realize that words have power and when you say something you are really speaking it into *being*. If you say you are poor, then you will be poor. If you say you are sick, then you will be sick. If you say your children are bad, then they will be terrible! You must speak good into your life and also speak about what you want your life to be! Scripture says that "we eat the fruit of our words" and also says that "blessings and curses are in the power of the tongue." So it is critical that you speak positive words and understand that your words have power!

What I loved about Deacon Walton's saying "Excellent!" is that I know from his life and our conversations, that his life had many challenges. He grew up in a time when there was a lot of discrimination. He grew up in a segregated area of the country, yet he overcame the challenges and lived a good life. Going through challenges—not getting his due and his recognition—yet making the decision to have an attitude of gratitude and great faith. When we talked, even as a older gentleman, he would share that everything was not always easy. **Yet he made a decision that it was going to be excellent.**

And that is why he was able to say "Excellent!" with such passion. And as a result, he started having a life of excellence.

So when you are going through your day and people ask you how you're doing, I encourage you to give a positive, enthusiastic, excited, and hopeful about your life response. Be excited about the way you want your life to go. Not what's happening right now, but what you want to happen. And you will see how that starts to impact how your life goes.

"Dr. Willie Jolley, how are you today?"

"I'm Excellent! Blessed and highly favored. Blessed, and grateful for each and every day."

You today make a decision to be *Excellent!*

Dr. Willie Jolley, CSP, CPAE is an amazing speaker, singer, author and media personality in one person. In 1999 he was named "One of the Outstanding Five Speakers in the World" & "Motivational & Inspirational Speaker of The Year" by Toastmasters International.

Many know him as the speaker Ford Motors called on in 2006 when they were on the brink of bankruptcy, and he worked with them in 2006, 2007 and 2008 and in 2009 they were able to reject a government bailout and go on to Billion Dollar profits.

In 2005 Willie Jolley was inducted into the prestigious Speaker Hall of Fame. In 2013 he was named "One of the Top 5 Leadership Speakers" by Speaking.com and in 2015 he replaced the legendary Zig Ziglar on the national Get Motivated Tour!

Dr. Jolley is the host of the #1 Motivational Show in America on Sirius XM and also hosts a daily radio show that precedes Steve Harvey's Morning Show. Dr. Jolley is the author of several international best-selling books including *It Only Takes A Minute To Change Your Life, A Setback Is A Setup*

For A Comeback, Turn Setbacks Into Greenbacks and *An Attitude of Excellence.*

Web: www.williejolley.com / Office: (202) 723-8863

* * * * * *

When I read articles, I seek to translate the material into memorable Life Hacks that I can use on a daily basis. So here are my interpretations of possible Life Hacks inspired by the above articles:

1. Own and maintain a *relaxed intensity*, which keeps everyone feeling confident.
2. Turn your words "I am going to" into benefits for your audience. (Example: "You will learn four specific ways that you can transform your organization.")
3. Be sure to accept good opportunities. Learn to accept the connections you make, knowledge you are offered, and offers for assistance.
4. You will get to decision points when it's necessary to take a risk. Move forward with the mindset "this or something better."
5. "Always be great"—that is, put kindness and compassion into what you do.
6. Start your day by choosing your attitude of "Excellent!"

List of 25 *Emotion-Motion Life Hacks:*

1. Energize by principles
2. Use feeling gratitude to lift your mood and empower your actions.
3. Replace worry with action.
4. Improve your personal brand.
5. Lead by forming good agreements.
6. Make your dream Bigger and more compelling than fear.
7. W – wake up the "Worst First"
8. I – intuit (Top Six Targets)
9. N – nurture 3 Levels of Goals
10. N – navigate by Goals – "Gold to Green"
11. E – energize and "See the 3"
12. R – run your own Triggers
13. Use pre-selected questions to turn the direction of your thoughts and feelings.
14. Open your thoughts to new possibilities: Think of what you can give, how you can go around obstacles and what else could be possible.
15. Consider taking a risk by answering vital questions.
16. For wealth: Focus on how can you build your business so you don't always have to be there.
17. Use Empowering Questions about how you can increase people's trust in you—to find new positive possibilities.
18. Set your own criteria for excellence.
19. Push aside fear and focus on your Voice of Intuition.
20. Improve your leadership: create a dialogue and ask questions.
21. Connect with your Want-Power and your intuition.

22. Remove limits by filling your life with that which empowers you.
23. Work it through: Write down details and explore the situation beforehand.
24. Focus on: Success is built on someone slamming their foot down on fear and stepping up.
25. Step Toward the Fear; Use Want-Power.

A Final Word and Springboard to Your Dreams

Congratulations on your efforts as your worked with the material in this book. To get even more value from this book, take the plans and insights that you created and place them in some form in your calendar or day planner. *Plan and take action.*

One of my speech topics is: **"Discover Your Enchanted Prosperity."**

I will share some brief insights here.

"When you enchant people, your goal [is] to fill them with great delight." – Guy Kawasaki

When I talk about *Your Enchanted Prosperity*, I'm referring to our uncovering that which delights us and other people. You discover how to serve people in ways that align with "what you're good at, what people will pay for and which *clients you want.*"

We'll use the O.N.E. process (as in *"you're the one* who knows in your heart."):

O – open

N – nurture intuition

E – encourage

1. Open

Many people are closed in their thoughts. You hear their comments like "That won't work."

Instead, I suggest that we focus on **"Let's find out!"** Pick useful sources of information and encouragement. Many people (including "experts") talk from looking in the rearview mirror—that is, from history.

Instead, *make plans and take action* as you test things and find out.

2. Nurture intuition

Think of your intuition as a friend who will help when you make time and space to *hear intuition.* We'd like intuition to inform us of the end game (steps 18, 19, 20) but intuition gives us Steps 1, 2, 3. When we complete Step 3— then intuition provides Steps 4, 5, 6.

To nurture your intuition, ask yourself, "Am I giving myself time to *tinker and listen*?" Frequently, in business, we do not have an immediate solution to a problem. If possible it helps to give ourselves some time (even one evening to "sleep on the problem"). Also talk with people and think through (or "tinker" with) the problem.

3. Encourage

To discover our *Enchanted Prosperity* path, we need to encourage ourselves. Do not wait for anyone's approval. Some people do not know how to give approval. Walt Disney did not wait for approval to make Disneyland. Steve Jobs did not wait for approval of all top music producers to offer songs at $0.99 each. In fact, the Beatles waited many long years before they finally made their songs available on iTunes.

As you do some experiments with projects, tell/ask yourself: *"Good effort. Good action.* What did I learn? Will I use this, refine it, or drop it?"

Additionally, it helps when your product/service *encourages* people to do new things and feel good as they do them. Steve Jobs insisted that iPod users needed to be able to get to their music in *three* clicks. Jobs led his team to make that possible. And iPod users felt good in getting fast access to their music.

To discover *Your Enchanted Prosperity* path, remember "Open, Nurture intuition and Encourage."

Meanwhile, return to the pages of this book again and again to reconnect with the material and take your life to higher levels.

The best to you,
Tom

Tom Marcoux
Executive Coach - Spoken Word Strategist

Special Offer Just for Readers of this Book:

Contact Tom Marcoux at tomsupercoach@gmail.com for special discounts on **coaching,** books, workshops and presentations. Just mention your experience with this book.

==> See an Excerpt from Tom Marcoux's book, *Darkest Secrets of Persuasion and Seduction Masters: How to Protect Yourself and Turn the Power to Good* – on the next page.

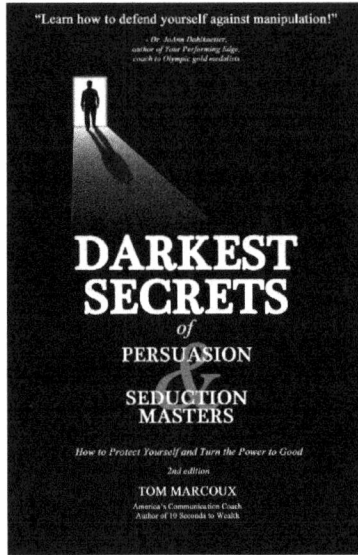

Excerpt from

Darkest Secrets of Persuasion and Seduction Masters: How to Protect Yourself and Turn the Power to Good

by Tom Marcoux, Executive Coach – Spoken Word Strategist
Copyright Tom Marcoux

. . . Now, I am in my 40's, with gray in my hair, and for 27 years I have been taking action to protect people.

And now is the time for me to protect you with the Countermeasures I reveal in this book.

Every human being needs to be able to break the trance that a Manipulator creates.

You need to make good decisions so you are safe and you keep growing—and you are not cut down and crippled.

This Darkest Secrets material is so intense that I first released it only with the counterbalance of my most energizing and uplifting books, *Nothing Can Stop You This Year!* and *10 Seconds to Wealth: Master the Moment Using Your Divine Gifts.*

An interviewer asked me: "Who can be the Manipulator?"

A co-worker, a boss, a salesperson, someone you're dating, and someone you think is a friend.

Now is the time—this very minute—for me to write this book to protect you.

I must speak the truth.

These Darkest Secrets of "persuasion masters" are …

Wait a minute! Let's say it plainly: These are the Darkest Secrets of masters of manipulation. Throughout this book, I will call these people what they are: Manipulators.

Dictionary.com defines "manipulate" as "To influence or manage shrewdly or deviously…. To tamper with or falsify for personal gain."

In this book, we will look on a manipulator as one who deviously influences someone with no concern about that person's well-being, and who causes harm to that person.

Here is the first Darkest Secret:

Darkest Secret #1:
Manipulators Make You Hurt
and Then Offer the Salve.

Manipulators would invite you to go out in the sun for hours and then sell you the salve to soothe your burns. The problem is that we don't notice that this is what they're doing.

For example, you're considering the purchase of a house. A Manipulator asks the question, "So, where would you put your TV?" This question is designed to put you into a trance.

Dictionary.com defines "trance" as "a half-conscious state, seemingly between sleeping and waking, in which ability to function voluntarily may be suspended." Let's condense this: in a trance you may not be able to function freely.

Here is the second Secret:

Darkest Secret #2:
Manipulators Put You into a Trance.

To protect yourself, you must learn to use Countermeasures to Break the Trance.

All the Countermeasures (actions you can take to break the trance) in this book will make you stronger and more capable of protecting yourself.

Now, we'll view the third Secret:

Darkest Secret #3:
Manipulators Care Nothing for You and Human
Decency: They'll lie, cheat, and do whatever they need
to do so they win—but their charm masks all this.

Let's return to the example of a Manipulator selling you a house. A Manipulator does not pause for an instant to see if you can truly afford the new house. The Manipulator would neglect to mention that you will not only have your mortgage payment of $900. There will be additional costs: home repairs, property tax, water, electricity, homeowner's insurance, and more. The Manipulator only emphasizes what he or she knows you want to hear: "Look! $900 is better than the $1500 you're paying for rent, which is just going down the toilet. And the $900 is an investment."

Let's go back to **Darkest Secret #1:**

Manipulators make you hurt and then offer the salve.

The Manipulator has you feeling good about the solution (salve) and feeling bad about your current life situation.

How? A Manipulator will make you hurt through questions such as:

• What bothers you about paying $1500 a month for rent? (The Manipulator will use a derisive tone when he says the word *rent*.)

• What is *not* smart about paying rent on someone else's house instead of investing in your own house?

• How do you feel about your children walking in the neighborhood where you live now?

Do you see how these questions are designed to make you hurt enough so that you'll buy?

An interviewer asked me, "Tom, aren't these good arguments for purchasing a house?"

"What we're looking at is the *intention* of the influencer," I replied. "Let's look at our definition of a manipulator as one who deviously influences someone with no concern about that person's well-being, and who causes harm to that person. If the person truly cannot afford the house, he or she will be harmed by buying it. If the manipulator conceals the truth, the manipulator is doing harm. That's the important difference."

Some friends of mine are ethical and helpful real estate agents who truthfully reveal the whole situation and help the purchaser achieve her own goals.

In this book, we are talking about another type of person; that is, unethical Manipulators.

* * *

In any given moment, we need to remember the tactics Manipulators use. We will focus on the word D.A.R.K. so you can remember details easily and protect yourself from Manipulators.

D — Dangle something for nothing
A — Alert to scarcity
R — Reveal the Desperate Hot Button
K — Keep on pushing buttons

1. Dangle Something for Nothing

What do conmen and conwomen do to seize your attention? They make you think you're getting a "steal."

I recently saw a documentary in which a conman on a street in England showed a toy that looked like it was dancing. This fake product was actually dancing because of a hidden, invisible thread. The conman was dangling something for nothing. The Entranced Buyer thought he was getting something worth $20 for only $5. That was the trick. The Entranced Buyer felt that he was getting $15 extra of value for his $5. What the Buyer really got was something worth nothing. Similarly, I know someone who purchased a copy of a Disney movie from a street vendor in San Francisco. She brought the copy home and it was unwatchable—and the street vendor was never seen again.

An old phrase goes, "A conman cannot con someone who is not looking for something for nothing."

How to Protect Yourself from "Dangle Something for Nothing"

Stop! Get on your cell phone and talk through the "deal" with someone you know who thinks clearly. Go home. Think about it. Do some research on the Internet. Listen to your gut feelings. If the salesman or conman is too insistent, get away from that Manipulator. Get quiet. Have a cup of water. Cool down. Break the Trance!

Break the Trance and Identify the Crucial Detail

Earlier, I mentioned that a Manipulator puts you into a trance. An added problem is that we put ourselves into a trance. For example, as you read this, are you thinking about your right toe? Most likely not (unless you stubbed your toe recently). The point is that we only focus on a tiny percentage of what is going on in our life.

Around fifteen years ago, I caused myself trouble because I put myself into a trance. I discovered that under certain conditions, friendship can make you nearly deaf. Here's how: I was producing a song for a motion picture. A good friend was singing backup in the chorus. Because of our friendship, I wanted him to sound great. I completely missed the Crucial Detail. In this kind of situation, the Crucial Detail is that what truly counts is how the lead singer sounds! I made a song that I could not release. What a waste of time and money! I had put myself into a trance.

In any situation in which the Manipulator is "dangling something for nothing," we often fall into a trance and miss the Crucial Detail. The most important detail is *not* that we're saving money if we order before midnight tonight. What counts is whether the product creates a lasting, crucial benefit in our lives. And is the benefit of the product worth the cost? Some people even program themselves to make mistakes by saying, "I can't pass up a bargain." The bargain is *not* the Crucial Detail.

Secrets to Break the Trance

This is the process of B.R.E.A.K.S. It will help you remember the proven methods to break a trance.

B — Breathe
R — Relax
E — Envision
A — Act on aromas
K — Keep moving
S — Smile

Secret #1: Breathe

Remember Secret #1: Manipulators make you hurt and then offer the salve. The Manipulator wants to put you into a state of being that fills you with a sense of urgency and anxiety. Oh, no! I'm going to miss the sale!

Stop this highly vulnerable state. Take a deep breath. Do it now. Take a deep breath and let your belly "get fat" by filling it with air. As you breathe out, let your belly deflate. Breathe in through your nose and breathe out through your mouth. This is called belly-breathing. Repeat the actions of belly-breathing three times. Good. Now, do you feel different? Remember, when you are relaxed, you are strong.

Secret #2: Relax

You become stronger when you condition yourself to relax in the face of adversity. Researchers note that when an Olympic athlete is confronted with the most stressful moment in her life, she has prepared in advance. She has given herself ways to calm down. Two powerful methods are described in this section about B.R.E.A.K.S. One is breathing, and the other is envisioning.

A special part of relaxing is the effective use of your posture. Many of us think that we're relaxed when we slouch. However, I was taught by three physical therapists that when you sit up and align your vertebrae, you are more relaxed because your back's bone structure is naturally supporting you. Many of us discover that placing a pillow behind the lumbar-area of our back helps us sit up better. If you are sitting or standing when talking with a Manipulator, ensure that your posture is aligned. You will have more power to protect yourself.

Secret #3: Envision

Envision an image that makes you feel strong. Often, our strongest images come from movies that we saw when we were young. Some of my clients envision being strong like Xena the Warrior Princess or Superman. One client thinks of Sean Connery as James Bond. Immediately, this client walks smoothly with poise. He feels confident. Act as if you are, and you are!

Also, envision yourself being quite aware of your surroundings. On vacation, many of us become entranced by our new surroundings. Travelers let their guard down. A conperson catches them at a weak moment. It's important to stay in the present and be alert to what's going on. Stay present with your needs, and shop around before making a large purchase. Be prepared to walk away.

Watch out for Manipulators who are slick, fast talkers. They try to get your money, and just minutes after they succeed, you realize what happened.

But this is *not* for you! You can remind yourself with an internal comment: "I am aware. What is really going on here?"

Secret #4: Act on Aromas

Let's notice the power of an aroma.

Smell is a potent wizard that transports you across thousands of miles and all the years you have lived. Helen Keller

Nothing is more memorable than a smell. One scent can be unexpected, momentary and fleeting, yet conjure up a childhood summer beside a lake in the mountains. – Diane Ackerman

You need to be able to calm down within seconds. One of

the fastest ways to do that is to use a favorite aroma. One of my clients has conditioned herself to calm down by smelling lavender. The process for her was to recline in a hot bath and smell lavender simultaneously. Now, the smell of lavender relaxes her limbs quickly.

Remember, when you are relaxed, you neutralize the Manipulator's tactic to make you feel that buying something now is an urgent matter. You let go of any anxious feelings the Manipulator seeks to create in you. Use an aroma to help you feel relaxed and strong.

Secret #5: Keep Moving

A trance often transfixes or freezes us, making us still. Sometimes, the most powerful way to break a trance is to use a movement that you prepared in advance. One of my clients closes his right fist and taps it on his right thigh. In his mind, he repeats the phrase: "I am my own person!" This helps him break out of a trance induced by a Manipulator.

Another client quietly snaps her fingers near her waist. This reminds her to "snap out of it."

End of Excerpt from
Darkest Secrets of Persuasion and Seduction Masters: How to Protect Yourself and Turn the Power to Good
    Purchase your copy of this book (paperback or ebook) at Amazon.com or BarnesandNoble.com
    See **Free Chapters** of Tom Marcoux's 31 books
    at http://amzn.to/ZiCTRj

ABOUT THE AUTHOR

You want more and better, right? Imagine fulfilling your Big Dream.

Tom Marcoux can help you—in that he's coached thousands of people: CEOs, small business leaders, graduate students (at Stanford University) speakers, and authors.

Marcoux is known as an effective **Executive Coach – Spoken Word Strategist.**

(and Thought Leader—okay, writing 31 books helped with that!)

** *CEOs, Vice-Presidents, Other Executives, Small Business Leaders:*

You know that leading people and speaking at your best can be tough.

Marcoux solves problems while helping you amplify your own Charisma, Confidence and Control of Time.

Interested? Email Marcoux—tomsupercoach@gmail.com

Ask for a *Special Report:*

* 9 Deadly Mistakes to Avoid for Your Next Speech

** *Speakers, Experts - for a great TED Talk, Book, Audio Book, Speeches, YouTube Videos.*

Marcoux solve problems while helping you to make your

Concise, Compelling Message that gets people to trust you and get what you're offering (product, service, *an idea*).

Yes - the *San Francisco Examiner* designated Tom Marcoux as "The Personal Branding Instructor."

Marcoux is an expert on STORY. He won a Special Award at the EMMY AWARDS, and he directed a feature film that went to the CANNES FILM MARKET and earned international distribution.

(Marcoux helps you "Be Heard and Be Trusted" . . . that's his 15th Anniversary, 3rd edition book.)

As a CEO, Marcoux leads teams in the United Kingdom, India and the USA. Marcoux guides clients & audiences (IBM, Sun MicroSystems, etc.) in leadership, team-building, power time management and branding. See Tom's Popular BLOG: www.TomSuperCoach.com

Specialties: coach to CEOS * Executives * Small Business owners * Leaders * Speakers * Experts * Authors * Academics

One of his *Darkest Secrets* books rose to #1 on Amazon.com Hot New Releases in Business Life (and in Business Communication). A member of the National Speakers Association for over 14 years, he is a professional coach and guest expert on TV, radio, and print.

Marcoux addressed National Association of Broadcasters' Conference six years running. With a degree in psychology, Tom is a guest lecturer at **Stanford University**, DeAnza, & California State University, and teaches business communication, designing careers, public speaking, science fiction cinema/literature and comparative religion at Academy of Art University. He is engaged in book/film projects *Crystal Pegasus* (children's) and *Jack AngelSword* (thriller-fantasy). See Tom's well-received blogs

at www.BeHeardandBeTrusted.com

at www.YourBodySoulandProsperity.com

Consider engaging **Tom Marcoux as your Executive Coach.**

"As Tom's client for many years, I have benefited from his wisdom and strategic approach. Do your career and personal life a big favor and get his books and engage him as

your Executive Coach." – Dr. JoAnn Dahlkoetter, author of *Your Performing Edge* and coach to CEOs and Olympic Gold Medalists

Tom Marcoux can help you with **speech writing** and **coaching for your best performance.**

As Tom says, *Make Your Speech a Pleasant Beach.*

Join Tom's Linkedin.com group: *Executive Public Speaking and Communication Power.*

At Google+: join the community "Create Your Best Life – Charisma & Confidence"

Get a **Free** report: "9 Deadly Mistakes to Avoid for Your Next Speech and 9 Surefire Methods" at

http://tomsupercoach.com/freereport9Mistakes4Speech.html

Tom Marcoux has trained CEOs, small business owners, and graduate students to speak with impact and gain audiences' tremendous approval and cooperation. *Learn how to present and get thunderous applause!*

"Tom, Thanks for your coaching and work with me on revising my speech at a major university. Working with you has been so enlightening for me. Through your gentle prodding and guidance I was able to write a speech that connects with the audience. I wish everyone could experience the transformation I have undergone. You have helped me discover the warm and compelling stories that now make my speech reach hearts and uplift minds. This was truly an empowering experience. I cannot thank you enough for your great assistance." — J.S.

"Tom Marcoux has been an NAB Conference favorite [speaker] for six years. And he is very energetic."

– John Marino, Vice President, National Association of Broadcasters, Washington, D.C.

"Using just one of Tom Marcoux's methods, I got more done in 2 weeks than in 6 months."
– Jaclyn Freitas, M.A.

Tom's Coaching features innovations:
- Dynamic Rehearsal
- Power Rehearsal for Crisis
- The Charisma Advantage that Saves You Time

Become a fan of Tom's graphic novels/feature films:
- Fantasy Thriller: *Jack AngelSword*
  type "JackAngelSword" at Facebook.com
- Science fiction: *TimePulse*
  www.facebook.com/timepulsegraphicnovel
- Children's Fantasy: *Crystal Pegasus*
  www.facebook.com/crystalpegasusandrose
- YA Fantasy: *Jenalee Storm*
  at Facebook.com – type "Jenalee Storm"

See **Free Chapters** of Tom Marcoux's 31 books
at http://amzn.to/ZiCTRj   Amazon.com

Your Notes:

_____

_____

_____

_____

Your Notes:

_____

_____

Space for Your Sketches related to Your Dreams:

www.ingramcontent.com/pod-product-compliance
Lightning Source LLC
Chambersburg PA
CBHW071904200326
41519CB00016B/4507